I0801655

Family Walks and Hikes in the Canadian Rockies

2nd Edition, Volume 2

Family Walks and Hikes in the Canadian Rockies

2nd Edition, Volume 2
Banff, Kootenay,
Yoho, Icefields Parkway
(Highway 93 North), Jasper

ANDREW NUGARA

RMB

Second Edition

For information on purchasing bulk quantities of this book, or to obtain media excerpts or invite the author to speak at an event, please visit rmbooks.com and select the "Contact" tab.

RMB | Rocky Mountain Books Ltd.
rmbooks.com
@rmbooks
facebook.com/rmbooks

Cataloguing data available from Library and Archives Canada
ISBN 9781771606226 (softcover)
ISBN 9781771606233 (electronic)

All photographs are by Andrew Nugara unless otherwise noted.

Printed and bound in China

We would like to also take this opportunity to acknowledge the traditional territories upon which we live and work. In Calgary, Alberta, we acknowledge the Niitsítapi (Blackfoot) and the people of the Treaty 7 region in Southern Alberta, which includes the Siksika, the Piikuni, the Kainai, the Tsuut'ina and the Stoney Nakoda First Nations, including Chiniki, Bearpaw, and Wesley First Nations. The City of Calgary is also home to Métis Nation of Alberta, Region III. In Victoria, British Columbia, we acknowledge the traditional territories of the Lkwungen (Esquimalt, and Songhees), Malahat, Pacheedaht, Scia'new, T'Sou-ke and W̱SÁNEĆ (Pauquachin, Tsartlip, Tsawout, Tseycum) peoples.

We acknowledge the financial support of the Government of Canada through the Canada Book Fund and the Canada Council for the Arts, and of the province of British Columbia through the British Columbia Arts Council and the Book Publishing Tax Credit.

Disclaimer

The actions described in this book may be considered inherently dangerous activities. Individuals undertake these activities at their own risk. The information put forth in this guide has been collected from a variety of sources and is not guaranteed to be completely accurate or reliable. Many conditions and some information may change owing to weather and numerous other factors beyond the control of the authors and publishers. Individuals or groups must determine the risks, use their own judgment, and take full responsibility for their actions. Do not depend on any information found in this book for your own personal safety. Your safety depends on your own good judgment based on your skills, education, and experience.

It is up to the users of this guidebook to acquire the necessary skills for safe experiences and to exercise caution in potentially hazardous areas. The authors and publishers of this guide accept no responsibility for your actions or the results that occur from another's actions, choices, or judgments. If you have any doubt as to your safety or your ability to attempt anything described in this guidebook, do not attempt it.

CONTENTS

Introduction vii
Area Map xvi

Banff 1
1. Cascade Ponds 4
2. Johnson Lake 6
3. Lake Minnewanka 8
4. Tunnel Mountain 10
5. Marsh Loop 13
6. Sundance Canyon 15
7. Bow River and Bow Falls 17
8. Sulphur Mountain 19
9. Fenland 23
10. Sunshine Meadows 25
11. Johnston Canyon 29

Kootenay National Park 35
12. Stanley Glacier 38
13. Marble Canyon 42
14. Paint Pots 44

Lake Louise 47
15. Lake Louise Shoreline 50
16. Plain of Six Glaciers 52
17. Lake Agnes / Mount St. Piran 56
18. Saddleback Pass / Fairview Mountain 63

Moraine Lake 69
19. Moraine Lake 71
20. Rockpile 73
21. Consolation Lakes 75
22. Larch Valley 78
23. Eiffel Lake 81

Yoho National Park 84
24. Paget Peak Lookout 86
25. Sherbrooke Lake 88

26. Takakkaw Falls 92
27. Yoho Lake 94
28. Iceline Trail 97
29. Laughing Falls 100
30. Emerald Lake 102
31. Wapta Falls 105

Icefields Parkway (Highway 93 North) 107
32. Helen Lake 110
33. Bow Lake and Falls 113
34. Peyto Lake Viewpoints 116
35. Bow Summit Lookout Site 120
36. Mistaya Canyon 124
37. Parker Ridge 126
38. Wilcox Pass 129
39. Forefield Trail / Toe of Athabasca Glacier 132
40. Tangle Falls 134
41. Beauty Creek 136
42. Sunwapta Falls 138
43. Athabasca Falls 140

Jasper 142
44. Valley of the Five Lakes 144
45. Path of the Glacier / Cavell Meadows 146
46. Old Fort Point Loop 148
47. Lake Annette 150
48. Maligne Canyon 152
49. Opal Hills 154
50. Bald Hills 158

Important Contacts 162
Acknowledgements 164
Disclaimer 165

INTRODUCTION

About *Family Walks and Hikes*

Personally, I cannot think of many better ways to bond as a family than to hike as a family. The physical, mental and emotional benefits of hiking are undeniable, and who better to share and reap those benefits with than the ones you love and cherish the most?

Families living near the Canadian Rockies are fortunate to be close to some of the best hiking routes the planet has to offer. This book describes some of the more popular trips in these mountains that are appropriate for kids of all ages, adding to the trips offered in *Family Walks and Hikes in the Canadian Rockies Volume 1*. So grab the kids, get in the car and enjoy!

The challenges of family hiking

Hiking with young people poses unique challenges. How do you pick the most appropriate trails for your family? (See **How the trails were chosen**, below.) How do you balance long driving times with fidgety bodies? And how do you keep kids motivated and moving once you are on the trail? The following are some tips that will help make your family hiking experience more enjoyable:

- Candy: While hiking, a treat every 10 to 15 minutes can provide the motivation kids need to keep moving.
- Bikes and Striders: Bring them whenever possible. Kids love to bike – it's no secret!
- Hiking games: Learn some hiking games for kids. Examples include I spy; scavenger hunts; follow the leader (with everyone taking turns as leader); red light, green light; I'm going on a picnic and other alphabet games; 20 questions; songs; and so on.
- Other families: Hike with another or multiple families. In general, kids love to hike with other kids.
- Water: The connection humans (especially kids) have with water is undeniable. Any trip that involves water (lakes, rivers, waterfalls, creeks, beaver ponds) is likely to be a hit with the young ones.

- Environmental Awareness: Whenever possible, educate your kids about the local environment and wildlife, and the benefits and responsibilities of hiking in the mountains (but don't beat them over the head with it).
- Bribes: A little bribery goes a long way. If kids know there is an ice cream run at the end of the hike, they are more likely to be motivated to keep going.
- Know Your limits: Know when to push kids and when it's time to give in. You can always try again another day.
- Backup: Have a backup plan – another hike or a different activity.
- Be patient, be patient and then be patient.

Getting there

See the area map on page xvi. Trips in this book encompass a large area, within the boundaries of four national parks: Banff, Kootenay, Yoho and Jasper. All destinations must be accessed by car.

Seasonal road closures

Road closures are unlikely to affect family hiking, as the restrictions occur in winter and spring. However, the closures are outlined below for those adventurous families that might want to hike in seasons other than summer.

- Highway 40 from December 1 to June 15, between Kananaskis Trail and Highwood Junction.
- Highway 66 from December 1 to May 15, west of Elbow Falls.
- Moraine Lake Road from mid-October to mid-May (may vary).
- Yoho Valley Road (Takakkaw Falls area) from October to mid-June.
- Cavell Road from October 15 to June 14 (may vary).

Facilities

Banff, Calgary, Canmore, Cochrane, Field (for Yoho National Park), Lake Louise (for Moraine Lake) and Jasper have all the amenities.

- Highway 1A (Exshaw): Heart Mountain Store (cafe, groceries, gas).
- Highway 1X (Bow Valley Provincial Park): small store at the Bow Valley campground.
- Highway 1 (Dead Man's Flats): gas, motel, small grocery store.
- Highway 93 North (Icefields Parkway): gas, restaurant, small store at the Saskatchewan River Crossing.

Weather

The best family hiking months in the Canadian Rockies are generally July, August and September. The temperature can reach the mid-30s in July and August, but it cools down quite a bit in September. Afternoon thunderstorms sometimes form during the hot months. Of course, snow can be expected in any month of the year but usually stays away in July and most of August. The different areas described in this book have slightly dissimilar hiking seasons and weather patterns:

- Banff experiences a July–September family hiking season that sometimes extends into October.
- Lake Louise, Moraine Lake, Yoho and Highway 93 North can have snow lingering well into July. An early-season snowfall will usually end the hiking season in early October. Routes in these areas are also prone to be cloudier than other places due to their location on or near the Continental Divide.
- Hiking in and around Jasper can be feasible by June, but in some years snow will linger well into July. In general the hiking season comes to a close in October.

What to wear

Hiking boots, as opposed to runners, are recommended for adults on most of the trails. However, appropriate gear may differ for young children. They are generally less susceptible to the types of ankle injuries that adults might sustain. And of course, children outgrow their footwear annually (sometimes monthly). A sturdy pair of runners with good tread will suffice for most of the routes described here. Kids who are up for more advanced trips, such as Fairview Mountain and Mount St. Piran, will need hiking boots with good ankle support. Bring a rain jacket and warm clothes, as the weather can change dramatically and very quickly. For those hot summer days, bring sunscreen, a hat and bug repellent.

Drinking water

To be safe, it is best to bring potable water from your home, hotel or campsite. Natural sources may be contaminated with *Giardia lamblia*, a parasite that can cause severe gastrointestinal problems. At higher elevations, it is generally safe to drink from streams without treating the water. Filtering water is also an option.

Wildlife concerns

Wildlife is abundant in every area described in this book. As exciting as it is for kids to see animals in their natural habitats, it is important that all hikers try to avoid wildlife encounters. Bears, moose, deer, elk, bighorn sheep and marmots are the most common types of wildlife you might encounter, but wolves, cougars and coyotes could also present themselves. When hiking, make lots of noise to warn bears and other wildlife that you are there. Moose and elk can be aggressive in the fall, during mating season – steer well clear if you encounter them.

Of course, feeding wildlife is a strict no-no. Please discourage this tempting but very harmful behaviour.

Another form of wildlife prevalent throughout the Canadian Rockies is the tick. From March to the end of June, ticks ravenously feed on any mammal they can sink their hooks into, humans included. Check yourself and your kids very carefully after any early season hike. DEET products (for your skin) and permethrin products (for your clothes) can be used to ward off these disease-ridden creatures.

Safety tips

A few pointers to help ensure your family experience is a safe and fulfilling one:

- Hike together, especially when your kids are younger.
- Don't be lulled into a false sense of security because you are in a larger group. You still must make noise to warn bears and other wildlife of your presence.
- Carry bear spray and know how to use it.
- Consider using a personal locator device, such as SPOT, in case of an emergency.
- Stay on designated trails unless you are experienced and/or familiar with the challenges of off-trail hiking/scrambling.
- Check the weather forecast before setting out. Also, check online resources and the designated park's visitor centre for trail conditions and trail and area closures.
- Afternoon thunderstorms are common in the summer. Start early to avoid them.

Campgrounds

Camping with kids can be a blast, a nightmare and everything in between. It is best to inundate them with camping experiences at a young age, so they get a feel for it and learn to love it.

Many campgrounds give easy access to the hikes described in this book. A few are listed here, but check the internet for a complete listing. Some campgrounds allow you to book online, but others operate on a first-come, first-served basis.

- Elbow Valley: Beaver Flats, Paddy's Flat, Little Elbow. Call 403.949.3132.
- Highway 40 north end and Bow Valley: Bow Valley Provincial Park. Call 1.877.537.2757 or reserve online.
- Highway 40 south end and Kananaskis Trail: Elbow Lake (backcountry). Call 403.678.0760 or book online. For Boulton Creek, Canyon, Elkwood, Interlakes and Lower Lake, call 403.591.7226.

- Banff, Kootenay, Lake Louise: Tunnel Mountain Village,
- Two Jack Lake, Johnston Canyon and Lake Louise. Book online for all.
- Highway 93 North: Mosquito Creek, Silverhorn Creek, Waterfowl Lakes, Rampart Creek (reserve online), Wilcox, Icefield, Jonas, Honeymoon Lake, Kerkeslin, Wabasso (reserve online). Unless otherwise noted, all are first-come, first served.
- Jasper: Snaring, Wapiti (reserve online), Whistler (family-oriented).
- Yoho: Hoodoo Creek, Kicking Horse, Monarch, Takakkaw Falls, Yoho Lake, Laughing Falls.

Using this book

How the trails were chosen

Choosing routes for family hiking is fraught with challenges. Driving time, trip length, elevation gain and quality of the trail are but a few of the many factors you must consider and scrutinize when attempting to determine if a route is a good candidate for a family hike. Add to that the wide range of fitness levels and abilities of children and accompanying adults, and you end up with a process that is far from an exact science.

The routes in this book are mostly short, already popular hiking trails. Preference has been given to routes that are varied and have multiple points of interest, which hopefully will keep kids (and adults) engaged and motivated. As much as possible, routes with options to extend the length of the trip have been chosen, so you can play it by ear and change the objective as you go. This also accommodates "advanced" family hikers who are used to longer and more strenuous trips. For example, if the objective is Larch Valley and the kids have no issues making it that far, you could extend the trip to include Sentinel Pass.

In picking a specific trip for your family, the adults in charge usually know best. You might have a 5-year-old who can hike every trail in this book without breaking a sweat or batting an eyelid. Conversely, your 10-year-old might struggle with even the easiest of trails. It is up to you to choose trips that best fit your family's abilities. On that note, it is always best to err on the side of caution and be conservative in choosing. As much as possible, I have tried to include short and longer hikes within short driving distances of one another, giving families the option to complete multiple hikes in one day if one hike is not enough. For example, after hiking the Stanley Glacier trail, you could drive down the road to see stunning Marble Canyon. Or, if you arrive at Moraine Lake and determine that the Larch Valley hike may be too much for your crew, the Moraine Lake shoreline hike is right there.

Trails

Parks Canada, Alberta Parks and other organizations have done an outstanding job of creating and maintaining the trails described in this book. Most of these trails are well marked and well signed. Therefore, many of the route descriptions in this book are brief, requiring very little detail. Even the routes without any signage are generally easy to follow.

Optional add-ons to extend your trip

Some trips in this book include optional add-ons: trips you can tack on to the main hike if you have the time and energy. Look for these **Going Farther** sections if your family usually has the stamina to combine adventures.

Location

This section provides the driving instructions you will need to get to the start of each trip, from Calgary.

Distance

Distances represent the round-trip distance for each trip.

Elevation gain

Elevation gain represents the total height gained for each round trip, including any significant ups and downs along the way.

Difficulty and age recommendations

Levels of difficulty in this book describe conditions underfoot and the steepness of trail grades. The difficulty rating assumes good hiking conditions, so bear in mind that adverse weather or snowy conditions may elevate the rating.

The age recommendations in the difficulty ratings should be considered general guidelines. Knowing your children's abilities and limitations is key. The recommendations assume children will be able to complete the entire trip on their own two feet. If you are carrying kids in baby carriers, the recommendations do not apply.

Season

Season describes the suggested times of the year to go on each hike. However, weather (specifically snow) can affect those suggestions quite dramatically. Areas farther west are especially prone to early snowfall that can render many routes off limits or at least unwise to travel on.

Of special interest for children

Included in this section of a trip description are recommendations for combining trips, chariot/jogging-stroller friendly trips, preferable time of year to undertake the route and other tidbits that may make the trip more enjoyable for the kids (and you).

Sketch maps

Red lines indicate main trails. Dashed red lines indicate optional routes and/or trip extension routes.

Do I need any other maps?

The maps provided for each trip provide all the information needed to perform the hike; there should be no need to carry other maps. However, for those who like to carry a complete map, NTS (National Topographic System) and Gem Trek produce excellent maps for all areas covered by this book. MEC, Atmosphere and many bookstores carry these maps.

If you would prefer a digital map, download the Topo Maps Canada app on your phone. The app uses a satellite signal, not a cell-phone signal, to pinpoint your exact location and then shows that location on a topographical map. Even if you are far out of cell-signal range, the app can still determine your location. The maps on Topo Maps Canada also show many of the trails in this book.

Doing more

If at some point in your family hiking journey you realize the family is ready for more challenging trips than the ones described in this book, pick up any or all of the following:

- the five volumes of *Gillean Daffern's Kananaskis Country Trail Guide*;
- other volumes in the *Popular Day Hikes* series;
- *Canadian Rockies Trail Guide*, by Brian Patton and Bart Robinson;
- *Classic Hikes in the Canadian Rockies*, by Graeme Pole;
- *Canadian Rockies Access Guide*, by John Dodd and Gail Helgason; and
- *Where Locals Hike in the Canadian Rockies*, by Kathy and Craig Copeland.

For those families who want to experience the Rockies year-round, consider cross-country skiing and snowshoeing trips. *Ski Trails in the Canadian Rockies*, 5th Edition, by Chic Scott and Darren Farley, and *A Beginner's Guide to Snowshoeing in the Canadian Rockies*, 2nd Edition, by Andrew Nugara, are great places to start.

The logical extension of hiking is scrambling – getting to the top of a mountain without technical means (i.e., ropes and climbing equipment). Generally this activity is for adults, but older children who show specific aptitude for advanced hiking may be up for it. For detailed information and route descriptions, acquire copies of Alan Kane's *Scrambles in the Canadian Rockies*, 3rd Edition, and *More Scrambles in the Canadian Rockies*, 3rd Edition, by Andrew Nugara.

AREA MAP

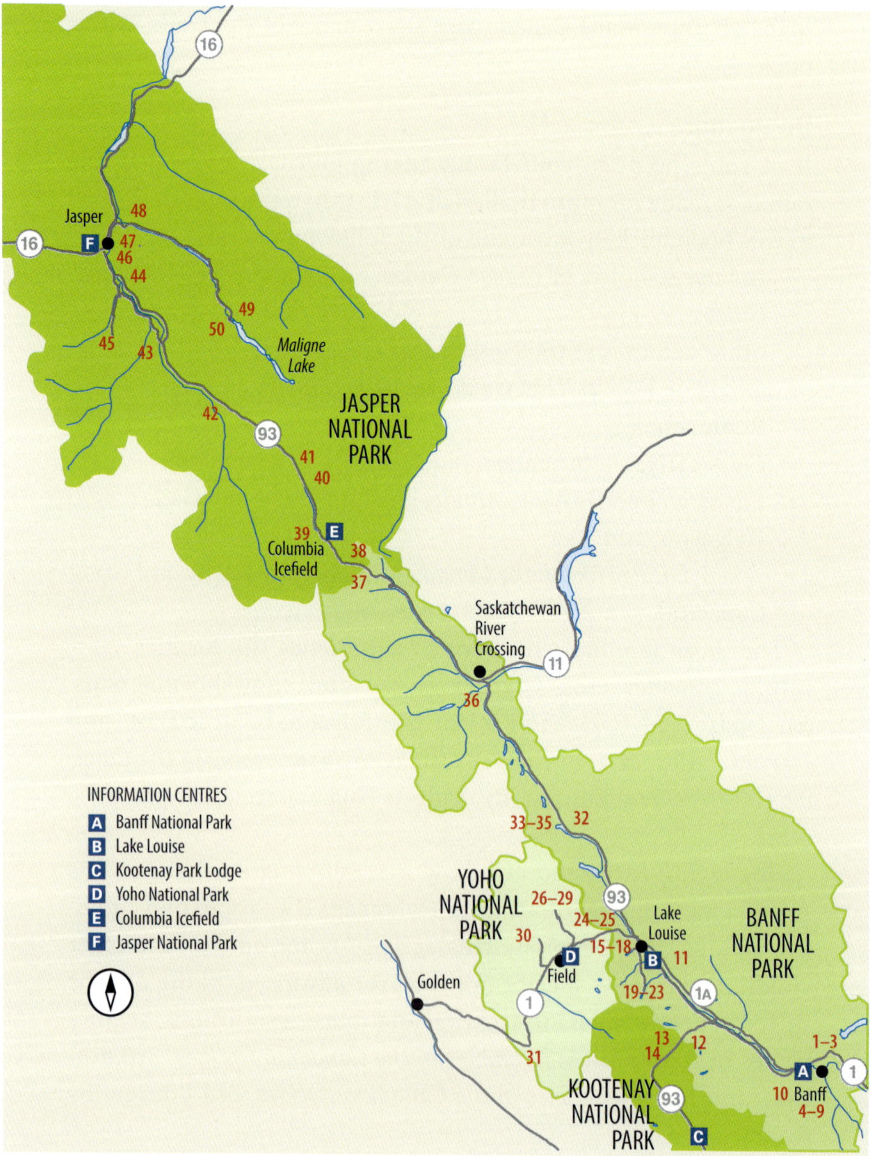
16
Jasper
48
47
46
44
45
43
49
50
Maligne Lake
JASPER NATIONAL PARK
42
93
41
40
39
Columbia Icefield
38
37
Saskatchewan River Crossing
11
36
33–35
32
YOHO NATIONAL PARK
26–29
93
24–25
Lake Louise
30
15–18
BANFF NATIONAL PARK
11
Field
Golden
1
19–23
1A
13
12
14
1–3
31
KOOTENAY NATIONAL PARK
93
10
Banff
4–9
1
INFORMATION CENTRES
A Banff National Park
B Lake Louise
C Kootenay Park Lodge
D Yoho National Park
E Columbia Icefield
F Jasper National Park

Banff

BANFF

Banff's lure for hikers involves the high number of easy, scenic hikes within short driving distances of one another, not to mention the townsite. No child can resist a visit to one of Banff's candy stores! Go for a hike or two, stop for dinner and then end the day with a dip at Banff Hot Springs – a perfect family outing.

Driving time from Calgary's city limits to the Banff townsite is about 1.25 hours. Parking can be difficult to find on busy summer weekends, so expect to walk a little. Note that all hikes in Banff, Kootenay Park and Lake Louise and along Highway 93, require you to have a park pass or day pass. Either can be purchased at the Banff National Park gates, a few kilometres west of Canmore on Highway 1.

PREVIOUS PAGE Family hiking also includes families about to grow, as Nicole Lisafeld proves. Husband Brian Vale and Mary the dog complete the picture.

Johnston Canyon, page 29, The Benbow family take a winter trip up Johnston Canyon (photo: Shawn Benbow).

1. CASCADE PONDS

Very short, but very interesting. Great views of Mount Rundle and Cascade Mountain and plenty of places to explore and then have a picnic.

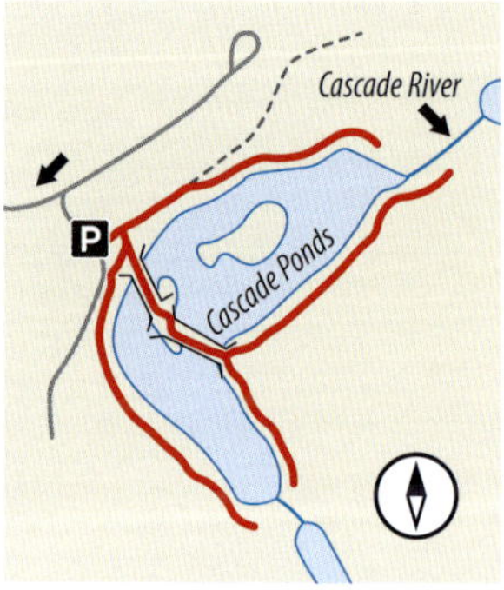

LOCATION

Drive west on Highway 1 and take the Lake Minnewanka turnoff (Exit 69). Follow the signs to Cascade Ponds.

DISTANCE

0.5 to 1 km return

ELEVATION GAIN

None

DIFFICULTY

Very easy, recommended for all; excellent paved and mud-packed trail throughout.

SEASON

Year round.

OF SPECIAL INTEREST FOR CHILDREN

After the hike, consider a drive farther up the road to Two Jack Lake for a dip in its cool waters, or a hike around Johnson Lake. In wintertime, this is a great place for fun in the snow. Stay on the trail, though.

1. Explore the trails and bridges as desired. The algae in the ponds can make everything look green!

FROM TOP Mount Rundle reflected in the green-tinged waters of the pond; the view of Cascade Mountain from the other side of one of the bridges; no "Bridge Over Troubled Water" here! (photo: Ruzel Jamilon).

2. JOHNSON LAKE

A relatively easy romp around a beautiful lake, with great views of Mount Rundle and Cascade Mountain.

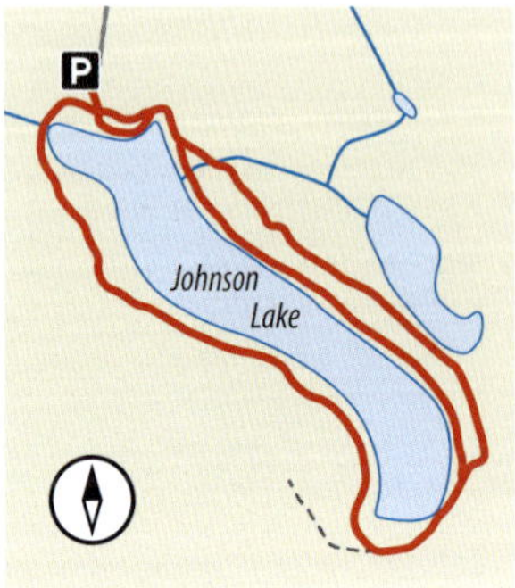

LOCATION

Drive west on Highway 1 and take the Lake Minnewanka turnoff (Exit 69). Follow the signs to Johnson Lake.

DISTANCE

3-km loop

ELEVATION GAIN

Minimal

DIFFICULTY

Easy, recommended for all; good trail throughout.

SEASON

Late spring, summer and early fall.

OF SPECIAL INTEREST FOR CHILDREN

The small beach at the northwest end of the lake is a great play/swim/raft area. Also, paddle boarding has become more popular on the lake. After the hike, consider a short drive farther up the road to Two Jack Lake for a quick hike around its western shore or for a swim.

1. Hike down to near the lakeshore and the picnic tables. The unsigned lakeshore trail starts here. Another trail that goes around the north side of the lake, but some distance away from it, and this trail joins up with the lakeshore trail later. Better to take the lakeshore trail from the beginning.
2. Turn left (northeast) and follow this trail in a clockwise direction. The trail is generally very easy to follow. It does veer

CLOCKWISE FROM TOP LEFT Ethan McDonough and Noah Koob take advantage of good weather at the Johnson Lake beach (photo: Tanya Koob); Noah Koob checks out the Billy Carver cabin, built in 1910 (photo: Tanya Koob); the famous swing on the north side of the lake (photo: Tanya Koob); if you are looking for some tranquility, you'll often find it at the southeast end of the lake; typical activity at the lake on a hot summer day.

away from the lakeshore at times, and at other times there is a bit of a drop off into the lake – watch your little ones!

3. Upon reaching the far (southeast) end of the lake, turn right, staying on the trail near the lakeshore as opposed to the outer trail. Hike this trail around the south side of the lake and back to the parking lot.

3. LAKE MINNEWANKA

One of the Canadian Rockies' most popular lakes. The area has lots of amenities and options to hike and explore.

LOCATION

Drive west on Highway 1 and take the Lake Minnewanka turnoff (Exit 69). Follow the signs to the Lake Minnewanka parking lot. Note that during high-traffic volume, a free shuttle to the lake is offered. To get to the shuttle parking lot, from just past the Lake Minnewanka turnoff, turn right towards Johnson Lake and look for the signed and large parking lot about 1 km along the road on the right.

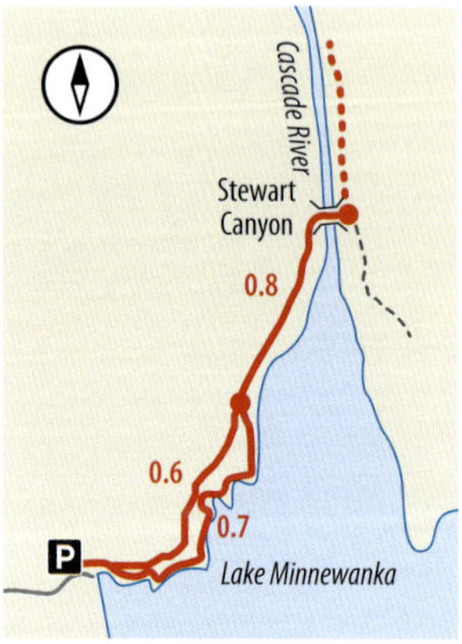

DISTANCE

1.2 to 2.8 km return

ELEVATION GAIN

50 m

DIFFICULTY

Easy along the trail, moderate along the lakeshore, and recommended for all. Excellent paved trail for a first 600 m and then a good mud trail to Stewart Canyon, and/or rocky and scrambly terrain near the lakeshore.

SEASON

Late spring, summer and early fall.

OF SPECIAL INTEREST FOR CHILDREN

The kids might like the fact that boat rentals and boat trips across the lake are available. They also might be interested in the availability of ice cream and other food items. Remember to yield right of way to cyclists and horses.

CLOCKWISE FROM TOP The rocky shoreline provides great views and lots of scrambling; the Boora family takes the fun-filled shoreline route (photo: Par Boora); kayaking around the lake is a great way to experience it from another perspective.

1. From the parking lot, walk down to the lake and follow the path that parallels the shoreline for 600 m to the signed Stewart Canyon trailhead. Alternatively (recommended), from the lake, follow one of the mud trails near the lakeshore. Scrambling the rocks near the water can be heaps of fun for the kids, but use discretion. A couple of small peninsulas provide great enjoyment for all. Stay near the water until you reach a pier, and then make your way onto Stewart Canyon Trail.

2. From the signed trailhead continue along the mud trail for 800 m to the bridge that spans Stewart Canyon. Travel beyond this point is not recommended. The trail that parallels Stewart Creek going upstream offers little in terms of interest, so I only recommend taking that trail if you need more exercise. Return the same way you came in.

4. TUNNEL MOUNTAIN

One of the easiest-to-reach official summits in the Canadian Rockies. Another potentially wonderful first summit for the kids.

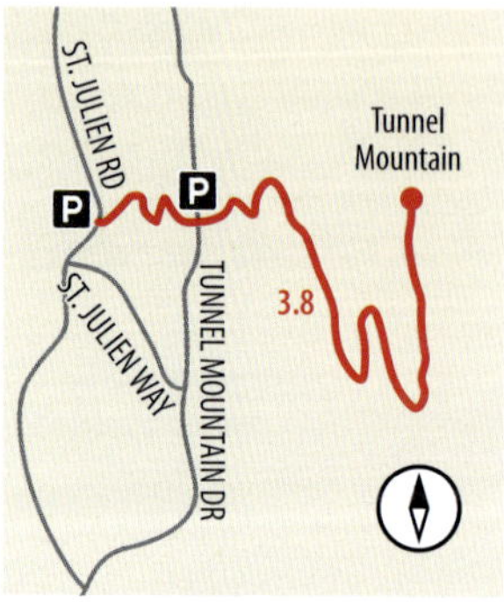

LOCATION

Drive west on Highway 1, take the Lake Minnewanka / Banff turnoff (Exit 69) and drive into Banff. Turn left onto Moose Street. Shortly after the road turns right, veer left onto St. Julien Road. Turn left onto St. Julien Way. Pass the unsigned lower parking lot (which you may need to return to) and turn left onto Tunnel Mountain Drive. Shortly, you will reach the upper parking lot, on the left side of the road.

DISTANCE

3.8 km return

ELEVATION

210–260 m; high point: 1690 m

DIFFICULTY

Moderate, recommended for children aged 4 and older; good trail throughout, with a few rocky sections. Fairly steep in some spots.

SEASON

Late spring, summer and early fall.

OF SPECIAL INTEREST FOR CHILDREN

The candy stores in Banff are a short drive away – a perfect post-summit treat. Note that the east face of the mountain sports numerous climbing routes, so DO NOT throw rocks down the mountain.

CLOCKWISE FROM TOP Uncle Bruce Watson guides Walter and James Benbow up the trail (photo: Shawn Benbow); Brianne and Penny Hobbs, with famous Mount Rundle in the background (photo: Matthew Hobbs); a couple of Adirondack chairs provide comfort for Mera Hobbs, 2, and Crux the dog while they enjoy views of the Banff townsite and Bow Valley corridor (photo: Matthew Hobbs); winter fun atop Tunnel Mountain with Matt, Mera, Brianne and Penny Hobbs (photo: "Nannie" Karen Christison).

"Nannie" Karen Christison fulfills her grandmother role of protecting the young (photo: Matthew Hobbs).

1. From the lower parking lot, follow the trail to the upper parking lot, cross Tunnel Mountain Drive to the signed trailhead and continue up the switchbacking trail towards the summit. From the upper parking lot, simply cross the road and follow the trail up.

2. Upon gaining the upper ridge, the best views of Mount Rundle can be experienced near the precipitous right side of the mountain. A metal fence provides some protection; however, getting through the fence would be not difficult, and any slip over the edge would be fatal. Watch the children carefully here – hand holding recommended. Also, again, remind everyone not to throw rocks down the side of the mountain, as climbers may be coming up the face.

3. From the viewpoint, continue to the top, where you are granted excellent views of the Banff townsite and the Bow Valley. Return the same way you came in. For safety reasons and to avoid damage to the fragile environment DO NOT try any shortcuts down the mountain.

5. MARSH LOOP

A relaxing trek alongside the famous Bow River, with two optional and interesting side trips from the Cave and Basin.

LOCATION

Head west on Highway 1, take the Lake Minnewanka/Banff turn-off (Exit 69) and drive into Banff, down Banff Avenue and over the Bow River. Turn right and follow the signs to the Cave and Basin parking lot.

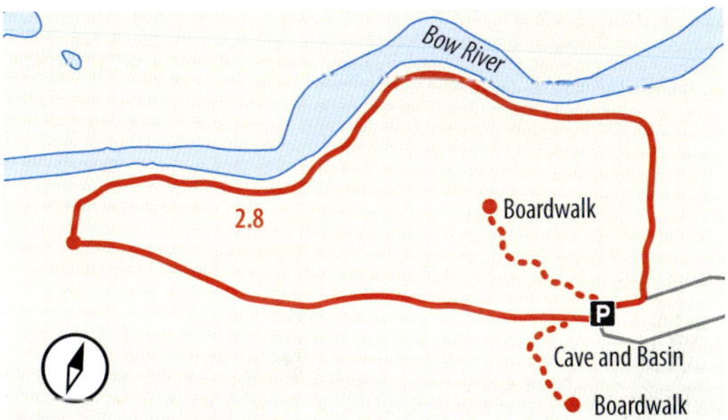

DISTANCE

2.8-km loop

ELEVATION GAIN

Minimal

DIFFICULTY

Easy, recommended for all. An excellent paved trail for the first section, good trail for the loop. This path is stroller-friendly when dry.

SEASON

Late spring, summer and fall.

OF SPECIAL INTEREST FOR CHILDREN

Visit the Cave and Basin National Historic Site before or after the hike – it's free with your annual park pass.

1. The wide, paved path goes past the Cave and Basin and then gradually loses elevation down to the valley.
2. Follow the path for about 1 km and then turn right at the Marsh Loop trail sign.
3. Hike the loop, taking in excellent views of the Bow River and surrounding mountains.

CLOCKWISE FROM TOP LEFT Nine months pregnant and still getting out to the mountains; Mary the dog, Brian and Nicole on the bank of the beautiful Bow River, where the final stretch of the hike grants good views of Mount Norquay; a curious youngster checks out the springs above the Cave and Basin; from the upper boardwalk, looking down on the Cave and Basin site, with Cascade Mountain behind (photo: Nicole Lisafeld).

4. The trail eventually takes a sharp turn to the right (south). Follow it straight back to the parking lot. Don't take the left turn as you near the parking lot.

5. Optional and highly recommended: The two boardwalk routes (one above the Cave and Basin and one below) are both interesting and educational.

6. SUNDANCE CANYON

Not quite the Grand Canyon, but wonderful nevertheless! The approach is great for bikes.

LOCATION

Drive west on Highway 1, take the Lake Minnewanka/Banff turn-off (Exit 69) and drive into Banff, down Banff Avenue and over the Bow River. Turn right and follow the signs to the Cave and Basin parking lot.

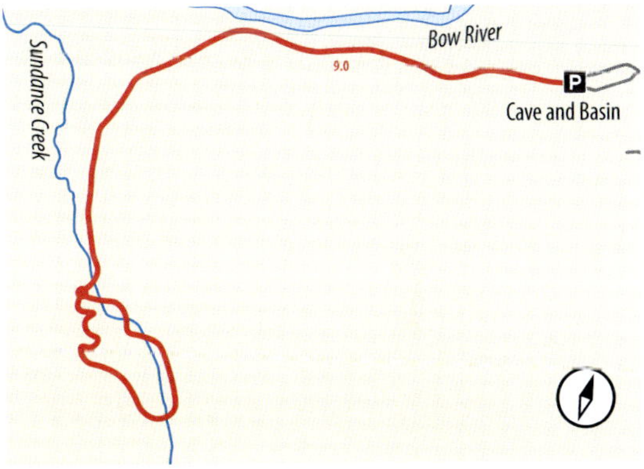

DISTANCE

9 km return

ELEVATION GAIN

155 m

DIFFICULTY

Moderately difficult, recommended for children aged 6 and older. The wide, paved trail to the canyon is good for bikes. There are steep rock steps to ascend in the canyon.

SEASON

Spring, summer and fall.

OF SPECIAL INTEREST FOR CHILDREN

An excellent bike and hike for the family. There is terrific water scenery throughout. Can easily be combined with Marsh Loop. The canyon may be too challenging for small children.

1. Hike or bike past the Cave and Basin and follow the wide, paved trail down to the valley and then alongside the Bow River. There are good views of Mount Edith's south spire.
2. This trail eventually veers left and continues up to Sundance Canyon (well signed). A bike rack is available if you rode in.

3. Hiking the fascinating Sundance Canyon is a much steeper and more challenging affair for the young ones. Cross the creek on a bridge and follow the increasingly steep trail up the canyon. Steep rock steps are a feature of the trail.

4. Gain the upper canyon and continue following the trail through the flatter, but equally interesting, narrow valley.

5. The trail eventually ends up on the right side of the creek and soon veers to the right and up. Don't miss this turn.

6. Shortly after, there is a hairpin turn in the trail that heads back to the start of the canyon. Follow the trail through forest.

7. When the trail seems to end at a wooden fence, it actually curves way over to the left. Enjoy the switchbacking trail back to the start of the canyon. If you biked the approach, the ride back to the Cave and Basin parking lot will be a blast!

8. Optional: When you reach the turnoff to Marsh Loop, turn left and follow the trail as described on page 13.

CLOCKWISE FROM TOP LEFT The Hobbs family have wisely chosen to bike the approach (photo: Matthew Hobbs); looking up from Sundance Canyon (photo: Karen Ung, playoutsideguide.com); Brianne and Mera Hobbs enjoying the upper part of the canyon (photo: Matthew Hobbs).

7. BOW RIVER AND BOW FALLS

Good views of a classic Banff landmark right from the start. This trail includes options for a very short trip or a longer one.

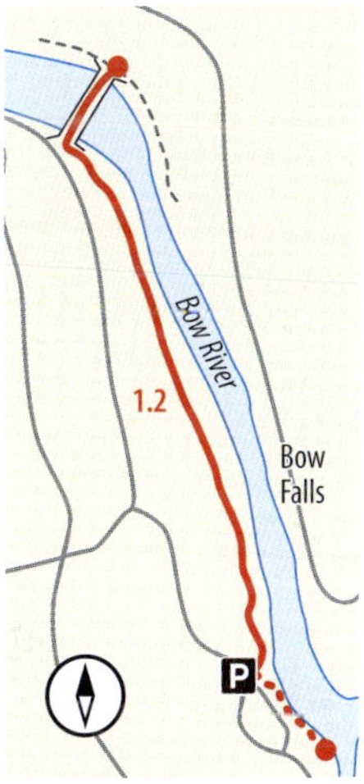

LOCATION

Drive west on Highway 1, take the Lake Minnewanka/Banff turnoff (Exit 69) and drive to Banff, down Banff Avenue and over the Bow River. At the end of the bridge, turn left and follow the signs to Bow Falls.

DISTANCE

2.4 km return

ELEVATION GAIN

Minimal

DIFFICULTY

Easy, recommended for all; excellent, paved path.

SEASON

Year round.

OF SPECIAL INTEREST FOR CHILDREN

Note that while Bow Falls is typically very crowded, the trail is less so.

1. Enjoy views of Bow Falls almost immediately, at the parking lot. Going a short distance downstream (no trail but easy travel along the riverbank) to where the Spray River pours into the Bow River offers interesting scenery and is entertaining for the kids.
2. After viewing the falls from various points, hike the paved trail up and upstream to the Bow Falls viewpoint a few minutes away. Return to the parking lot or continue along the trail.

CLOCKWISE FROM TOP Taking a well-deserved rest and enjoying the vista over the Bow River to Cascade Mountain (photo: Ruzel Jamilon); the view of Mount Rundle from above the falls is a pretty good one too; Bow Falls in winter; Bow Falls as seen from the trail above.

3. If you continue along the trail after the viewpoint, you will come to a footbridge over the river. Go as far as you would like. The middle of the footbridge does make for a fine viewpoint. Explore the area as desired and then return the same way you came in.

8. SULPHUR MOUNTAIN

A long, forested hike to one of the most popular destinations in Banff.

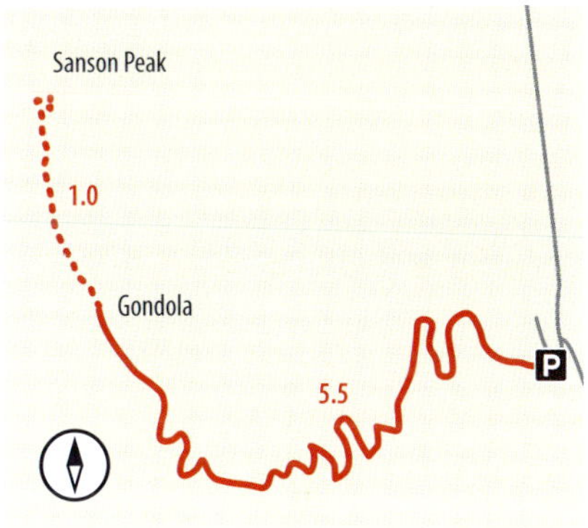

LOCATION

Drive west on Highway 1, take the Lake Minnewanka/Banff turnoff (Exit 69) and drive to Banff, down Banff Avenue and over the Bow River. At the end of the bridge, turn left and follow the signs to the Sulphur Mountain Gondola. The parking lot and trailhead appear as the road turns sharply to the right.

DISTANCE

11 km return

ELEVATION GAIN

655 m; high point: 2200 m

DIFFICULTY

Very strenuous, recommended for children aged 10 and older; good trail throughout, but up relentless switchbacks.

SEASON

Late spring, summer, early fall.

OF SPECIAL INTEREST FOR CHILDREN

Fun for the kids. A possible incentive to keep hiking: the free ride down on the gondola from October 10 to May 18 (as of 2018). As well, Banff Hot Springs is right up the road from the trailhead. Take your swimwear (but leave it in the car for the hike). Note that winter ascents are possible but not recommended, due to avalanche concerns.

FROM TOP The wonderful panorama to the west; four Hobbses at the top; the view from inside the gondola centre. (Top and bottom photos: Matthew Clay; middle photo: Matthew Hobbs.)

1. The trail is easy to follow and well signed. Find the trailhead at the northwest end of the parking lot and follow it up seemingly endless switchbacks to the summit. There are a couple of signed left turns you don't want to miss.
2. At the top, make your way onto the Sulphur Mountain platform and take in the views. Don't expect solitude here! There is an interpretive centre, restaurants and a gift shop inside – plenty to keep the kids occupied. Return the same way you came in, continue along to Sanson Peak (short and highly recommended) or take the gondola down (check for rates; may not be an option during peak periods; free from October 10 to May 18).

Going Farther: Sanson Peak (Cosmic Ray Station)

An easy interpretive boardwalk to the excellent viewpoint at the northwest end of the mountain. A must-do if you are already on Sulphur Mountain.

Distance

Add 2 km return

Elevation gain

Add 50 m; high point: 2256 m

Difficulty

Easy from the Sulphur Mountain platform, recommended for children aged 6 and older.

1. Follow the boardwalk to the now defunct Cosmic Ray Station (active in studying cosmic radiation from 1957 to 1978). Views are excellent. Return the same way you came in.

FROM TOP Noah Koob, 6, walks the boardwalk to the Cosmic Ray Station (photo: Tanya Koob); lots to look at from the station, including Cascade Mountain, the town of Banff and the Bow River snaking down the valley; looking back to the gondola and the true summit of Sulphur Mountain.

9. FENLAND

A forest- and creek-side interpretive trail that's easy for the whole family.

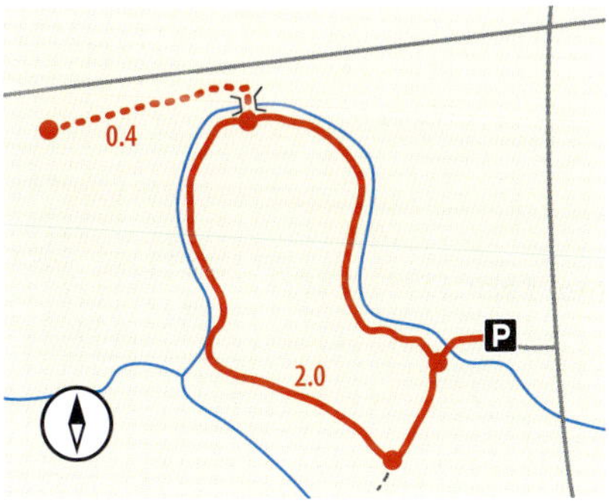

LOCATION

Drive west on Highway 1, take the Norquay/Banff turnoff (Exit 65), head towards Banff and take the second right after the turnoff into the unsigned parking lot. The trailhead is marked at the west end of the parking lot.

DISTANCE

2-km loop

ELEVATION GAIN

None

DIFFICULTY

Easy, recommended for all; good trail throughout.

SEASON

Late spring, summer and early fall.

OF SPECIAL INTEREST FOR CHILDREN

Bikes work well, but don't go too fast – there are many blind corners. After completing the hike, a drive down the Vermilion Lakes Road can be very rewarding. There are several piers the kids can go out onto and the views of Mount Rundle are spectacular. Another option for the family is to rent canoes or kayaks from the Banff Canoe Club (corner of Wolf Street and Bow Avenue) and sail the waterways around Fenland and into the Vermilion Lakes.

1. From the trailhead, hike the trail over a bridge and then, in a clockwise loop, follow the Fenland trail signs. Pleasant creek scenery and a few open views along the way make the hiking pleasant.

CLOCKWISE FROM TOP Vermilion Lakes Road offers spectacular views of Mount Rundle; kayaking and canoeing are popular on the gentle water; Noah Koob, 6, bikes the loop (photo: Tanya Koob).

Going Farther: First Vermilion Lake

For some extra exercise – adding 800 m return – and potentially great views of Mount Rundle reflected in the first Vermilion Lake, look for the sign to Vermilion Lakes posted about two-thirds of the way around the loop. Turn left (north) onto the trail, cross a bridge, go to the Vermilion Lakes Road and hike west alongside the road for about 400 m to a pier overlooking the lake. The kids will likely want to go to the end of the pier. Take some photos and return the same way you came in. To see the remaining lakes in the group, it is best to drive to each, via Vermilion Lakes Road. The lakes sport several piers, awesome viewing points, wildlife and the mountains, and interpretive panels describing the geology of this wetland area.

10. SUNSHINE MEADOWS

An exciting trip for the family that starts with a gondola ride (or bus ride) followed by a chairlift to the top. The environs of the "meadows" are sublime.

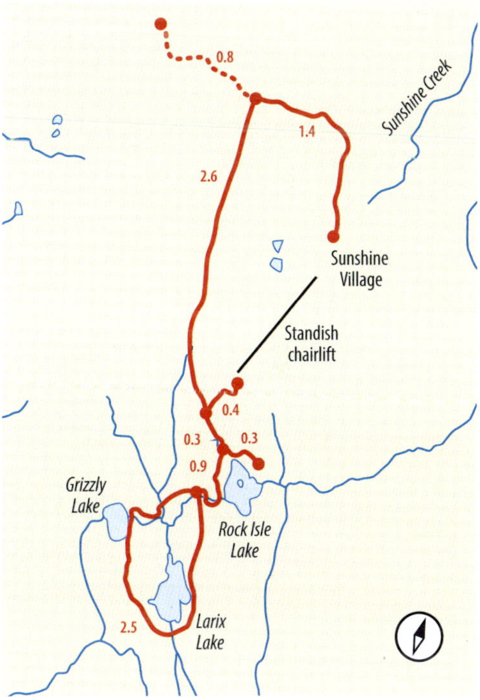

LOCATION

Drive west on Highway 1, past Banff. Take the Sunshine turnoff and follow the road 7 km to the Sunshine gondola.

DISTANCE

11.3-km loop

ELEVATION GAIN

160 m; high point: 2305 m

DIFFICULTY

Moderate, recommended for children aged 4 and older. Excellent trail throughout. Be sure to always stay on the trail.

SEASON

Summer and fall.

OF SPECIAL INTEREST FOR CHILDREN

There are many points of interest the kids will love, including tons of watery scenery, wildflowers by mid-July and far-reaching views. Check the internet for gondola ride prices ($59 adults, $29 children 6–15, free for toddlers 0–5 as of 2022). Bus rides are also offered on certain days. Sunshine Village has many amenities, including a lodge if you want to stay the night. Pick and choose your route. The description here is for the complete route.

1. Take the gondola up to Sunshine Village (20 minutes), grab a map at the top and then take the Standish chairlift to the high point of the day. With a map in hand, detailed instructions are not required, but the following is the suggested route to experience the area.
2. From the top of the chairlift, hike a short distance to the Standish Viewpoint for a fine view of the two lakes you will be visiting.
3. Hike 400 m down to an intersection and turn left towards Rock Isle Lake.
4. Another intersection is soon reached, but it is best to keep going straight to the Rock Isle Viewpoint on the northeast side of the lake.
5. Backtrack to the aforementioned intersection and turn left onto the trail that leads to the Larix Loop trail. Hike 900 m to the start of the loop.
6. Hike the 2.5-km Larix Loop trail in a clockwise direction. At the lake, views of the Monarch are terrific. The loop then continues on to Grizzly Lake and then to the Simpson Viewpoint. Although partially blocked by trees, Simpson Viewpoint offers a terrific view of the valley and the results of a forest fire.
7. Return to the first junction you reached. Instead of returning to the Standish Viewpoint, take the Twin Cairns to Monarch Lookout Trail going north. Hike 2.6 km to another signed junction.
8. Turn left and hike easily to the fine Monarch Viewpoint. If motivated, complete the extension described below in **Going Farther**, or return to the signed junction and then complete the loop via Meadow Park Trail. I'm sure the kids will want to pop into the Sunshine Village complex for treats at the end! Take the gondola back to the start.

FROM LEFT Grandpa Bill Wong and Mia Skogen on the Standish chairlift (photo: Amy Wong); Greg Jones and daughter Leah hike towards Rock Isle Lake (photo: Stacey Jones).

Going Farther: Simpson Pass

Some additional hiking for additional scenery around the Monarch Viewpoint.

Distance

Add 1.6 km return

Elevation

Add 80 m on return

Difficulty

Strenuous, recommended for children aged 8 and older. Good trail throughout.

1. From the Monarch Viewpoint, continue on the trail towards Simpson Pass, losing elevation all the way.
2. Hike the trail for about 800 m until you arrive at a beautiful little stream characterized by orange-coloured rock. Stop here, cool off in the stream and then return to the Monarch Viewpoint. Going all the way to Simpson Pass is not very rewarding from a scenery standpoint and therefore not recommended.

FROM TOP **Sunshine Meadows, page 25.** More terrific scenery below Monarch Viewpoint; there *is* ice cream at the end as sisters Mera and Penny Hobbs share a tasty treat at Sunshine Village (photo: Matthew Hobbs); stop here and then return to the viewpoint.

11. JOHNSTON CANYON

Possibly the most popular and crowded hike in the Canadian Rockies, but deservedly so.

LOCATION

Drive west on Highway 1, past the Banff turnoffs, and turn right onto Highway 1A (Exit 59). Follow the highway to one of the Johnston Canyon parking lots.

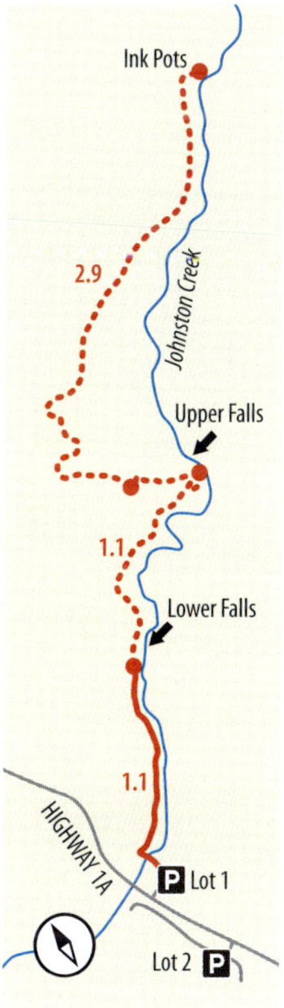

DISTANCE

2.2 to 11.6 km return

ELEVATION GAIN

50–135 m

DIFFICULTY

Easy to Johnston Creek's lower falls, recommended for all; moderate to the upper falls, recommended for children aged 4 and older. Paved trail all the way.

SEASON

Late spring, summer and early fall.

OF SPECIAL INTEREST FOR CHILDREN

Although the path is chariot/jogging-stroller friendly, chariots can cause congestion on the busy narrow sections, so using them is not recommended. Remind your children to walk in single file wherever possible. Expect large crowds, and be patient and considerate. Remember to allow faster travellers to pass you. Finally, and perhaps more important, usually ice cream is available at the bottom of the trail.

FROM TOP Note the tunnel through the rock that leads to another, closer viewpoint of the falls: if you are tall and/or have an infant on your back, duck! (photo: Amélie Doucet); typical crowds at the lower falls; the Benbow family at the upper falls (photo: Shawn Benbow).

1. If you parked in the second parking lot, hike to the first parking lot. From parking lot 1, go over the bridge and find the trail on the other side, which goes up Johnston Creek.
2. Follow the path and catwalks for 1.1 km to a viewpoint of the lower falls. Crossing the bridge and going through a small tunnel to a closer viewpoint may be the highlight for many kids.
3. Consider walking a very short distance up the upper falls trail, where you will get a different perspective of the lower falls. Return the same way you came in or continue to the upper falls.

Going Farther: The Upper Falls

A much steeper affair than the lower falls, but still on a good, mostly paved trail.

Distance

Add 3.2 km return

Elevation gain

Add 200 m

Difficulty

Moderate, recommended for children aged 4 and older.

From the first viewpoint of the lower falls, follow the signs and trail to the upper falls. Be sure to visit both viewpoints once you get there – one at the base of the falls and the other above the falls.

Going Farther: Ink Pots

This add-on is for the older kids who have a little stamina for elevation gain.

Distance

Add 5.8 km return

CLOCKWISE FROM TOP LEFT The Ink Pots (the different hue of each pool is due to how fast the pool fills: slower filling means greater suspension of fine silt particles that absorb different wavelengths of light (photo: Tanya Koob); the upper falls (photo: Katy Emanuel); a wonderful group of young people from the U.S. taking in the great scenery at the Ink Pots.

Water bubbling up from beneath the ground causes circles to form in the quicksand.

ELEVATION GAIN

Add 200 m; high point: 1645 m

DIFFICULTY

Strenuous, recommended for children aged 7 and older.

1. From the upper falls, follow the signs for the Ink Pots. There is only one signed junction, about 200 m up the trail, from the first sign. Turn right at this junction.
2. Follow the trail to a high point and then down into the valley that holds the Ink Pots – a group of five small but colourful spring-fed pools with basins composed of quicksand.
3. To protect this fragile environment, be diligent about staying on the trail as you explore. Return the same way you came in.

CLOCKWISE FROM TOP Lake Minnewanka, page 8, heading out onto one of the peninsulas; **Johnson Lake, page 6**, Two Jack Lake – another Rockies beauty; **Sulphur Mountain, page 19**, the view to the west is not too shabby: one of the Canadian Rockies' most famous peaks, Mount Temple, is visible in the distance; **Bow Falls and Trail, page 17**, David Emanuel accompanies his son Gavin, 2½, down the stairs above Bow Falls (photo: Katy Emanuel).

Kootenay National Park

KOOTENAY NATIONAL PARK

From Calgary's city limits, travel time to this part of the Rockies is between 1.5 and 1.75 hours. Amenities are limited, but a stop in the town of Banff will allow you to stock up before your hike or get a treat on the way back.

The Paint Pots and Marble Canyon hikes are short, interesting and easy to complete one right after the other – both are highly recommended. Stanley Glacier appeals to the more seasoned hiker with good stamina.

PREVIOUS PAGE The Paint Pots is one of the most unique trips in the book, fascinating for kids.

CLOCKWISE FROM TOP LEFT **Paint Pots, page 44**, the Nugara clan at the large pool at the end of the trail; **Marble Canyon, page 42**, a couple of places at the side of the trail are perfect spots for kids to hone their scrambling skills; **Stanley Glacier, page 38**, Dan Carreiro heads up the left side of the valley, aiming for the treed plateau in the centre.

12. STANLEY GLACIER

See the regrowth of the forest after a major fire in 2003, a beautiful hanging valley, waterfalls and of course Stanley Glacier. A favourite hike for many.

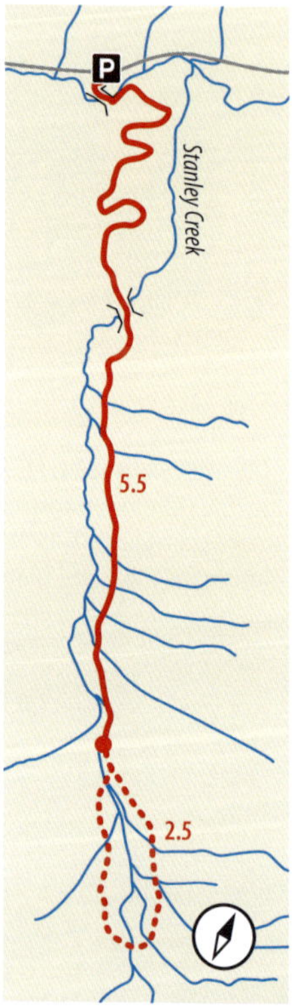

LOCATION

Drive west on Highway 1. About 25 km past Banff, take the Highway 93 South turnoff (Exit 35) towards Radium. Drive 13 km to the Stanley Glacier parking lot on the left (east) side of the highway.

DISTANCE

11 km return

ELEVATION GAIN

365 m; high point: 1920 m

DIFFICULTY

Moderately strenuous, recommended for children aged 7 and older who have stamina; good trail for the first half, but rockier on the second half, with more challenging footing.

SEASON

Summer and early fall.

OF SPECIAL INTEREST FOR CHILDREN

Wildflowers can be spectacular here from mid- to late July. You can combine this trip with a visit to Marble Canyon and/or the Paint Pots (see following trips).

1. From the trailhead sign at the south end of the parking lot hike the easy-to-follow trail for 5.5 km to the signed end of the route, enjoying occasional views of the cascading waters of Stanley Creek, the luscious green of forest regrowth (after

CLOCKWISE FROM TOP Dan Carreiro arrives at the end of the official trail; Brianne Hobbs carries Mera Hobbs, 9 months, up the lower section of the Stanley Glacier trail (photo: Matthew Hobbs); Kiran and Paula Boora check out the regrowth of the forest that was decimated by a 2003 fire (photo: Par Boora).

several destructive fires) and the tremendous walls of Stanley Peak on the right side of the valley.

2. At the end of the trail there are plenty of big rocks to rest on and have a lunch break. Return the same way or continue to the upper valley (see **Going Farther: The Upper Valley** below).

Going Farther: The Upper Valley

Get much closer to the Stanley Glacier on this trail, which affords stunning views on a clear day. Recommended only for those who are comfortable on loose, rocky, steep terrain.

Distance

Add 2.5 km return

Elevation gain

Add 200 m

Difficulty

Very strenuous, recommended for children aged 10 and older.

1. From the end of the official trail at the boulders, trails on both sides of the valley create a possible loop route that ascends one side of the valley up to the treed plateau near the Stanley Glacier and then descends the other side of the valley, back to the end of the official trail. The recommended route is the trail on the north side of the valley on ascent, giving you the option to descend the same way or make it a loop. Also, the trail on the north (left) side of the valley is generally better and allows for almost immediate views of the glacier. That route is described here.
2. After resting at the boulders for a spell, continue up the valley on one several primitive trails through the boulder field, looking for the obvious trail to the left (north). Once you're on that trail it is difficult to go wrong.
3. Follow the trail across the side of the slope all the way up to the sparsely treed plateau. Most will call this their high point. Either return the same way you came in or, from the treed plateau, continue following the trail (faint at times) around to the other side of the valley. Depending on the time of year, this may require an easy stream crossing.
4. This trail hugs the impressively steep walls of Stanley Peak (passing a few waterfalls that become ice climbs in the winter) and then descends to the valley, back to the boulder area. From there, return the same way you came in.

FROM TOP Just above the treed plateau is gorgeous glacial scenery (photo: Dan Carreiro); as you head back down, the view of Mount Whymper keeps you entertained.

13. MARBLE CANYON

A short but super-interesting and scenic trip, perfect for the whole family.

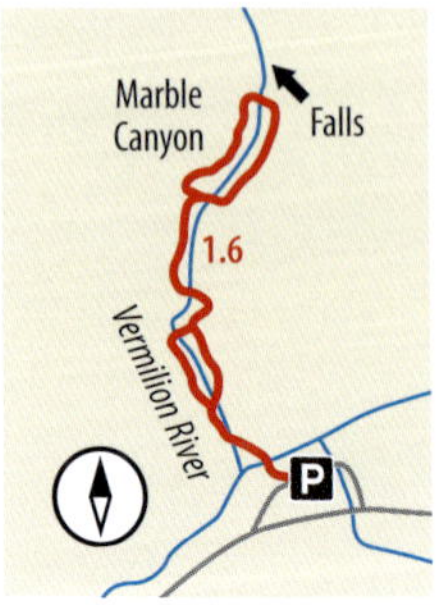

LOCATION

Drive west on Highway 1. About 25 km past Banff, take the Highway 93 South turnoff (Exit 35) towards Radium. Drive 17 km to the Marble Canyon parking lot on the right (west) side of the road.

DISTANCE

1.6 km return

ELEVATION GAIN

50 m

DIFFICULTY

Easy, recommended for all; excellent trail throughout with only one section of steep stairs.

SEASON

Year round, but much trickier in the winter.

OF SPECIAL INTEREST FOR CHILDREN

Hand-hold the little ones for safety in this canyon. If the kids are up to it, you can combine this trip with a visit to the Paint Pots and/or Stanley Glacier.

1. The Marble Canyon trail is well signed, easy to follow and does not require a detailed description. It begins with a steep staircase of rock that leads to a consistently high-quality trail. Watch the kids carefully throughout. Although fences prevent direct access to the canyon, there are many places where little ones could sneak through, especially on the bridges over the canyon.

CLOCKWISE FROM LEFT The steep staircase of rock near the beginning is the toughest part of the trip; a couple of places at the side of the trail are perfect spots for kids to practise their scrambling skills; 2-year-old Skye Nugara could easily sneak under the railing here – hold those hands; the end of the canyon and of the trail. Going out onto the rocks by the creek is not recommended for kids.

14. PAINT POTS

One of the more unique and colourful hikes in the book. Lots to keep the kids entertained.

LOCATION

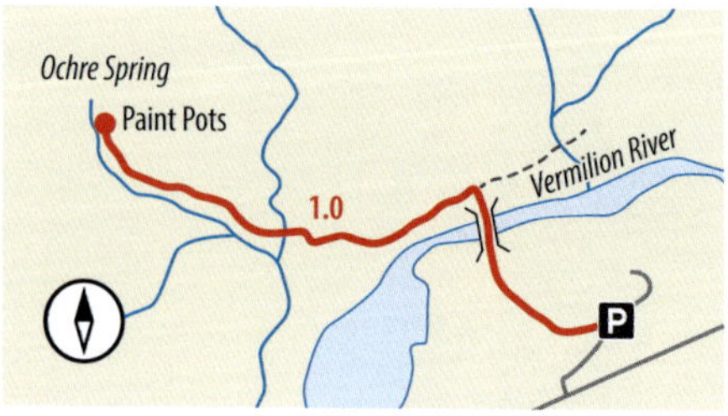

Drive west on Highway 1. About 25 km past Banff, take the Highway 93 South turn-off (Exit 35) towards Radium. Drive 20 km to the Paint Pots parking lot on the right (west) side of the road.

DISTANCE

2 km return

ELEVATION GAIN

Minimal

DIFFICULTY

Easy, recommended for all; good trail all the way. Stay on the trail to avoid damaging the fragile environment.

SEASON

Late spring, summer and early fall.

OF SPECIAL INTEREST FOR CHILDREN

This trail is almost chariot/jogging-stroller friendly. Be prepared to lift the chariot up and down the steps to the bridge. Remind your children to stay on the trail throughout. Combine this trip with a visit to Marble Canyon and/or Stanley Glacier if you have the stamina.

1. From the trailhead, obviously leading from the parking lot, hike about 300 m down to the Vermilion River and cross it on the bridge.

FROM LEFT Use the planks along the trail to avoid damaging the environment; stay on the trail as Rogan and Kian Nugara, ages 6 and 3, are making sure they do.

2. Turn left (south) and follow the trail through light forest into a more open area that marks the beginning of the Paint Pots. You will immediately notice that the colour of the ground is a little unusual.

3. Follow the increasingly vibrantly coloured trail/boardwalk through the area, eventually coming out alongside a small stream. STAY ON THE TRAIL THROUGHOUT this fragile environment. The kids may want to go off trail but do prevent them. This is a good time for your best "protect and cherish the environment" lesson.

4. Interpretive trail signs, old artifacts from a mining operation, a few pools of water and, of course, the orange-tinged and iron-rich soil are highlights of the trip.

5. You know you have reached the end of the line when you arrive at an open area with a large pool at the end. The trail does continue but offers little in terms of scenic rewards until you've persevered for several kilometres up the valley. Go for the extra exercise if desired. Otherwise, return the same way you came in.

Marble Canyon, page 42, the beautiful waterfall at the end of the canyon.

Lake Louise

LAKE LOUISE

Driving time to Lake Louise from Calgary's city limits is approximately two hours. Lake Louise is deservedly one of the most popular destinations in the Canadian Rockies. Expect tons of amazing scenery, but not solitude, and not necessarily a parking space either. Free shuttles run from the Lake Louise overflow parking lot (5.5 km east of Lake Louise on the south side of Highway 1) to Lake Louise during the summer months. This may be your best bet on busy summer weekends. If weekday trips are possible for you, that's the way to go.

The easiest and best introduction to the area is the classic Lake Louise shoreline hike. The option to continue along to experience the stunning environs around the Plain of the Six Glaciers exists from the end of this hike.

Reaching the summit of Fairview Mountain and/or Mount St. Piran make for great long-term goals for your family as the children develop and improve as hikers. The ascents are great, both with breathtaking views.

The Lake Louise Samson Mall offers some amenities for hikers, including a supermarket, a book store and an outdoor shop.

PREVIOUS PAGE The Dewit family at the summit of Fairview Mountain (self-timed photo: Vern Dewit).

CLOCKWISE FROM TOP **Lake Agnes / Mount St. Piran, page 56**, from the small col another "invisible" trail winds its way up the summit block; **Saddleback Pass / Fairview Mountain, page 63**, the wonderful summit panorama (photo: Vern Dewit); **Plain of Six Glaciers, page 52**, it's a colour explosion of Hobbses at the lakeshore! (photo: Matthew Hobbs); **Lake Louise Shoreline, page 50**, the ice sculptures (and the Ice Castle not seen here) – are terrific; **Saddleback Pass / Fairview Mountain, page 63**, sisterly love at Saddleback Pass (photo: Matthew Hobbs).

15. LAKE LOUISE SHORELINE

Explore one of the most picture-perfect lakes in the Rockies, perhaps in the world!

LOCATION

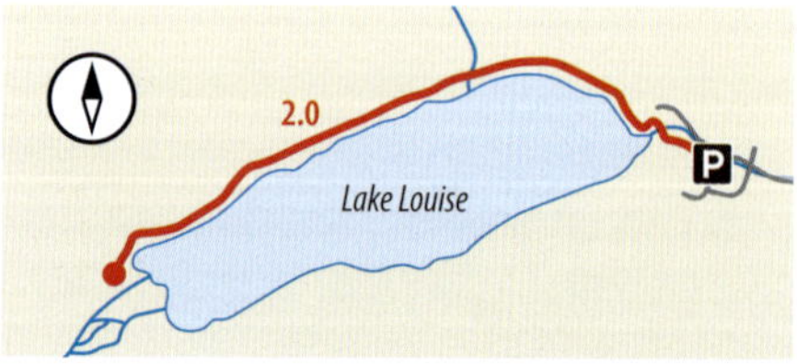

Drive west on Highway 1, take the Lake Louise turnoff (Exit 10), and follow the signs to the Chateau Lake Louise public parking lot. Note that this parking lot often fills up before 9 a.m. on summer weekends (see the introduction to this section for information about the free shuttle that runs from the overflow parking lot during the summer months).

DISTANCE

4 km return

ELEVATION GAIN

None

DIFFICULTY

Easy, recommended for all; excellent trail all the way.

SEASON

Year round.

OF SPECIAL INTEREST FOR CHILDREN

For weekend trips, arrive very early and expect huge crowds. After the hike, consider renting a canoe and exploring the lake via the water. Be sure to make the kids do all the paddling! Winter trips to the lake can be very rewarding for families, with activities like ice skating, cross-country skiing, snowshoeing and viewing the beautiful ice sculptures that abound here.

CLOCKWISE FROM TOP LEFT The classic view of Lake Louise from near the head of the lake; some take the trail, some take the rocks – Keira Collins, 14, and Rogan Nugara, 6, went for the rocks; the lake is alive with winter activities when it freezes.

1. From the parking lot make your way to the lake.
2. Hike 2 km around the right (north) side of the lake to the far, southwest end. On warm summer days, you can watch climbers ascend the magnificent quartzite cliffs. Return the same way you came in or continue up to the Plain of the Six Glaciers (next trip).

16. PLAIN OF SIX GLACIERS

An incredibly scenic extension of the Lake Louise shoreline hike.

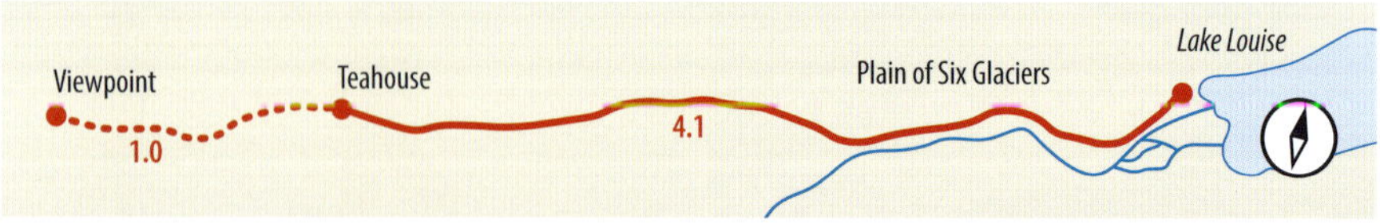

LOCATION

Drive west on Highway 1, take the Lake Louise turnoff (Exit 10), and follow the signs to the Chateau Lake Louise public parking lot. Note that this parking lot often fills up before 9 a.m. on summer weekends (see the introduction to this section for information about the free shuttle from the overflow parking lot that runs during the summer months).

DISTANCE

14.8 km return

ELEVATION GAIN

365 m; high point: 2070 m

DIFFICULTY

Strenuous, recommended for children aged 8 and older; good trail, with a couple of narrow, exposed sections.

SEASON

Summer, early fall.

OF SPECIAL INTEREST FOR CHILDREN

Recommended for older children, due to the overall length and terrain. But there is a tea house for refreshments at the end of the trail (bring cash) – a nice enticement. Note that snow can persist here into July, making travel more challenging for early-season trips.

You might meet climbers on their way to the north summit of Mount Victoria (photo: Mark Nugara).

1. After hiking to the west end of Lake Louise (see **15. Lake Louise Shoreline** above), continue along the trail up to the valley above. Follow the signs for the Plain of Six Glaciers Tea House.

2. About one kilometre farther, the terrain opens and the forest gives way to glacial moraine. In about another kilometer, the trail narrows considerably, with a steep drop on the left. A cable has been secured to the rock for extra protection against a fall. Watch the children carefully here. If this section is too dangerous, back up a short distance and find a signed horse trail that traverses below the steep section. This trail completely avoids the exposed main trail but joins up with it shortly after.

3. Follow the trail up to the tea house and stop in for bite to eat and maybe a drink. Explore the area around the tea house. There are some interpretive signs, benches, a few minor trails and of course plenty of views. Return the same way you came in or continue the trip to the Deathtrap Viewpoint (see **Going Farther: Deathtrap Viewpoint** below).

Fall colours and Mount Lefroy – an unbeatable combination (photo: Matthew Hobbs).

Going Farther: Deathtrap Viewpoint

The awe-inspiring views of a classic Rockies glacier: the Deathtrap, also known as Victoria Glacier. Recommended only for older kids.

Distance

Add 2 km return

Elevation gain

Add 130 m; high point: 2225 m

Difficulty

Difficult, recommended for children aged 10 and older.

Continue following the trail for another 1.5 km to a viewpoint of the famous "Deathtrap" – the steep tongue of Victoria Glacier known for avalanches and deep, hidden crevasses. The trail loses elevation and then regains it alongside the moraine of the glacier, eventually ending when the terrain gets too steep. Enjoy the view of the Deathtrap leading up to Abbott Pass, mounts Aberdeen, Lefroy and Victoria and The Mitre, and then return the same way you came in.

CLOCKWISE FROM TOP Coming up the moraine (photo: Brigid Meegan Scott); Brianne Hobbs near the end of the line (photo: Matthew Hobbs); winter trips can be stunningly gorgeous, but are extremely strenuous.

17. LAKE AGNES / MOUNT ST. PIRAN

Start at one stunning lake and end up at another – a great trip for the whole family.

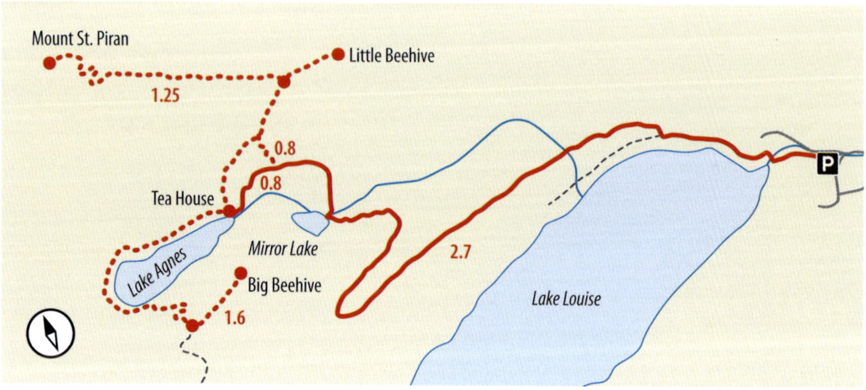

LOCATION

Drive west on Highway 1, take the Lake Louise turnoff (Exit 10), and follow the signs to the Chateau Lake Louise public parking lot. Note that this parking lot often fills up before 9 a.m. on summer weekends (see the introduction to this section for information about the free shuttle from the overflow parking lot that runs during the summer months).

DISTANCE

7 km return (Lake Agnes)

ELEVATION GAIN

400 m; high point: 2135 m

DIFFICULTY

Strenuous, recommended for children aged 6 and older; excellent trail all the way.

SEASON

Summer and early fall.

CLOCKWISE FROM TOP At Lake Agnes, early morning trips are often rewarded with relative solitude and stunning lake reflections – note the Devil's Thumb rock formations at the left, for those **Going Farther: Big Beehive**; a small waterfall immediately below Lake Agnes and Big Beehive (photo: Vern Dewit); Big Beehive above Mirror Lake (photo: Vern Dewit).

Misty morning view from Little Beehive.

OF SPECIAL INTEREST FOR CHILDREN

The kids will love the yellows of larch season here. Make sure you go early to avoid the crowds. Finally, entice your kids to persevere with the promise of refreshments at the Lake Agnes Tea House.

1. From the parking lot, make your way to the lake via the connecting trail and start hiking around the right (north) side of the lake. Find the signs for Lake Agnes and follow the relatively gently graded trail for 2.7 km to the first stop at Mirror Lake.
2. After checking out Mirror Lake, return to the Lake Agnes trail and follow it for 0.8 km to Lake Agnes, passing a signed junction for Little Beehive along the way. Keep following the signs to Lake Agnes. Upon arriving, you will encounter the tea house immediately; it sits at the far east end of the lake.
3. Either go back the same way you came in or extend the trip by hiking around the right (north) side of the lake to the west end. Here, you will be treated to an excellent view of the lake and the surrounding mountains. From the west end there is also a trail that heads west, up into the stunning valley under mounts Niblock and Whyte. Follow that for as long as desired and then return the same way you came in.

Great self-timed photo with Brigid Meegan Scott and Mark Scott, taken by Brigid, on the way to Little Beehive.

Going Farther: Little Beehive

A little extra exercise with a few fantastic views along the way.

Distance

Add 2.2 km return

Elevation gain

Add 105 m; high point: 2240 m

Difficulty

Strenuous, recommended for children aged 9 and older.

1. From near the tea house follow the signs for Little Beehive. No need to backtrack to the junction you passed on the way up. Also, if you intend to do St. Piran after Little Beehive, remember where the St. Piran trail sign was, about halfway to Little Beehive.
2. The best views occur shortly after that trail sign. Look for an open area to the right (south) where you can venture out onto the rock. There is a significant drop, so hold on to the young ones. The views across the valley are awesome.

3. From the end of the trail (at a decommissioned fire lookout) wander around a little for various views. Return the same way, initially, but you don't have to go back to Lake Agnes. Follow the signs for the alternative trail back down to Mirror Lake and out. Mount St. Piran is also an option from Little Beehive: remember that trail sign noted in step 1.

Going Farther: Mount St. Piran

A serious summit with a seriously amazing view! Recommended only for older kids with sturdy footwear.

Distance

Add 5.7 km return from Lake Agnes

Elevation gain

Add 500 m from Lake Agnes; high point: 2633 m

Difficulty

Very strenuous, recommended for children aged 12 and older.

1. From Lake Agnes, follow the signs to Little Beehive for about 500 m.
2. Look for a trail sign that informally marks the Mount St. Piran trail (as of 2018, "St. Piran" was scribbled on the official sign with felt pen). Turn left onto this trail and follow it westward for about 10 minutes through forest to Mount St. Piran.
3. The trail very neatly switchbacks up the entire mountain. Before the final ascent, you will arrive at the small col, with a terrific view to the north and east.
4. Follow the trail all the way to the expansive summit. The three lakes (Agnes, Louise and Mirror) are not visible from the summit, but a short loss of elevation towards Lake Louise reveals a stunning view of all three. Return the same way. There is an alternative descent route via the St. Piran / Niblock col, but it is NOT recommended for families.

Getting this view of the three lakes requires some minor elevation loss to the southeast.

Going Farther: Big Beehive

A scenic jaunt around the lake and then up to a decent viewpoint above it.

Distance

Add 3.2 km return

Elevation gain

Add 135 m; high point: 2270 m

Difficulty

Strenuous, recommended for children aged 9 and older.

1. From Lake Agnes, follow the signed trail around the right side of the lake to the south shore and then up steep switchbacks to the col between Big Beehive and Devil's Thumb, the distinctively shaped rock formation west of Big Beehive.
2. Turn left (east) and head for the shelter at the top of Big Beehive. Trees block some of the views, but moving around the summit lets you take it all in. Return the same way you came in or take the alternative route back down to Mirror Lake as indicated by the signs.

CLOCKWISE FROM TOP The Hobbs clan hike around Lake Agnes; a little wandering at the top can yield some great views (both top photos: Matthew Hobbs); the panorama of the outrageously beautiful Lefroy and Victoria; sweet golden larches line the switchbacks (both bottom photos: Vern Dewit).

18. SADDLEBACK PASS / FAIRVIEW MOUNTAIN

A scenic and steep grind to a beautiful pass and the gateway to one of the finest viewpoints in the Rockies, atop Fairview Mountain.

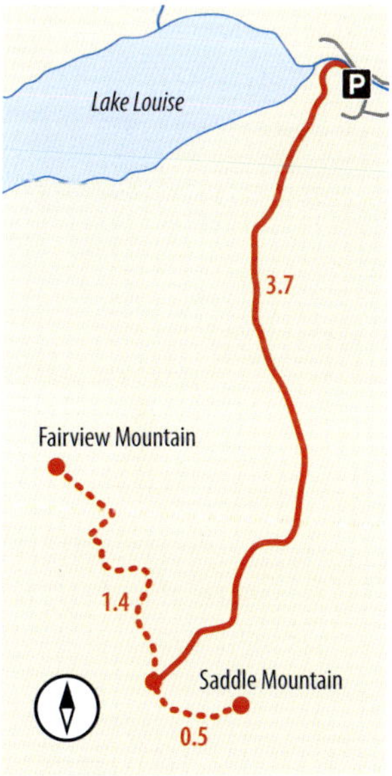

LOCATION

Drive west on Highway 1, take the Lake Louise turnoff (Exit 10), and follow the signs to the Chateau Lake Louise public parking lot. Note that this parking lot often fills up before 9 a.m. on summer weekends (see the introduction to this section for information about the free shuttle from the overflow parking lot that runs during the summer months).

DISTANCE

7.4 km return (Saddleback Pass)

ELEVATION GAIN

595 m; high point: 2315 m

DIFFICULTY

Strenuous, recommended for children aged 8 and older; good trail up to the hanging valley. Steep, rocky trail to the summit of Fairview and Saddle Mountain.

SEASON

Summer and early fall.

OF SPECIAL INTEREST FOR CHILDREN

Lots of larches grow at the pass, so late-September trips can be super-scenic. There are options to reach the summit of Fairview Mountain and/or Saddle Mountain if Saddleback Pass is not enough for you and the kids.

Niko, 8, and Hanneke Dewit on the Saddleback Pass trail, with Kaycie Dewit, 10, leading the way (photo: Vern Dewit).

1. From the parking lot, make your way to the lake and find the trail sign for Saddleback Pass on the left (northeast) side of the lake.

2. The route to the pass is well signed and easy to follow. Gaining the pass to the sight of Sheol Mountain and the beautiful Haddo Peak can be a wonderful experience. Return the same way you came in or continue along to Fairview Mountain and/or Saddle Mountain per the **Going Farther** suggestions below.

Going Farther: Fairview Mountain

With over 1000 m of elevation gain from the Lake Louise parking lot, this is the toughest ascent in the book for kids. It also sports perhaps the best summit view of any trip in the book – pick a clear day!

Distance

Add 2.8 km return from Saddleback Pass

Elevation

Add 410 m; high point: 2744 m

Mera Hobbs, 4, and mum take the final few steps to Saddleback Pass (photo: Matthew Hobbs).

Difficulty

Very strenuous, recommended for children aged 12 and older.

Of special interest for children

Recommended for older children, due to the overall length, significant elevation gain and rocky terrain. Sturdy footwear is a must. Snow can remain on the ascent slopes into July. Go later in the summer to avoid travel on snow.

1. From Saddleback Pass, the route up Fairview Mountain, to the northwest, is obvious and easy to follow. A good trail goes all the way to the summit. Monitor the kids carefully on this one and make sure they will be comfortable descending the steep and sometimes loose trail.
2. Take in the spectacular summit view and then return the same way you came in. True masochists will run up Saddle Mountain once back at Saddleback Pass.

Kaycie Dewit, 10, leads the way up Fairview Mountain (photo: Vern Dewit).

Going (Even) Farther: Saddle Mountain

Saddle Mountain can be easily ascended in conjunction with Fairview or as an alternative to Fairview if that ascent is too much for the kids. The view pales in comparison to that from Fairview but is still outstanding.

Distance

Add 1 km return from Saddleback Pass

Elevation gain

Add 130 m; high point: 2433 m

Difficulty

Strenuous, recommended for children aged 10 and older.

1. From Saddleback Pass, the route up Saddle Mountain, to the east, is also obvious (see photo). Gain the ridge and then follow it to the summit. Do not stray too far to the right (south), as huge rock bands line the south face. The rocky terrain does make this ascent a little challenging for younger kids.
2. Enjoy the terrific view of Mount Temple, Sheol Mountain and Haddo Peak and then return the same way you came in.

CLOCKWISE FROM TOP LEFT Noah Koob, 2 at the time, knows good rock when he lies on it – awesome quartzite! (photo: Tanya Koob); what a view – Danica Marks and Anibel Erickson, both 10 (back row), Abishai Erickson, 8 (middle), with Noah Koob, 7, Esme Erickson, 6, and Sebastian Marks, 8 (front) have good reason to celebrate this achievement (photo: Alyssa Erickson); Saddle Mountain as seen from near Saddleback Pass – the easiest ascent route goes around to the right (photo: Vern Dewit).

CLOCKWISE FROM TOP LEFT **Lake Agnes / Mount St. Piran, page 56**, looking back across the lake from the west end; **Lake Louise Shoreline, page 50**, Rogan Nugara, 6, and Keira Collins, 14, rock-hopping along the lakeshore; **Saddleback Pass / Fairview Mountain, page 63**, winter ascents of Saddle can be breathtaking, but are considerably more dangerous due to avalanches – you'll have to wait until you have AST (avalanche skills training) 1 or 2, kids; **Lake Agnes / Mount St. Piran, page 56**, stunning view of mounts Niblock and Whyte from the summit of St. Piran.

Moraine Lake

MORAINE LAKE

Battling it out with Louise, Bow, Peyto, Kananaskis and Spray for lake supremacy in the Canadian Rockies is Moraine Lake – a deep-turquoise-hued body of water surrounded by a group of spectacular mountains known as the Valley of the Ten Peaks. No written description can ever prepare you for the sheer beauty of this lake.

Unfortunately, Moraine Lake, even more so than Lake Louise, has succumbed to the pitfalls of popularity, the most frustrating being accessibility. At present (2022), your options for getting to the lake during the summer months are to arrive at the parking lot before 5:30 a.m. or pay $8 each to take a shuttle from the Lake Louise overflow (8 a.m. – 4 p.m.). An online reservation system is available at banfflakelouise.com/explorethepark/lake-louise-moraine-summer-shuttle. The fee, in my opinion, is absolutely worth it. Expect large crowds at the lake and on most of the trails. Before you go, check for hiking restrictions due to bear activity.

Driving time from the Calgary city limits is usually at least 2.25 hours. Allow extra time if you are taking the shuttle. At the lake, Moraine Lake Lodge offers refreshments and meals. If your wallet is bursting at the seams, there is the option to stay at the lodge!

PREVIOUS PAGE Easy to see why Moraine Lake is a Canadian Rockies treasure.

19. MORAINE LAKE

Combine with the Rockpile to get the most out of your Moraine Lake experience.

LOCATION

Drive west on Highway 1 to Lake Louise and follow the signs to Moraine Lake. Note that the parking lot fills up as early as 6 a.m., even on summer weekdays. On a busy weekend, the shuttle from the Lake Louise overflow is your best bet ($8 each, but price may vary).

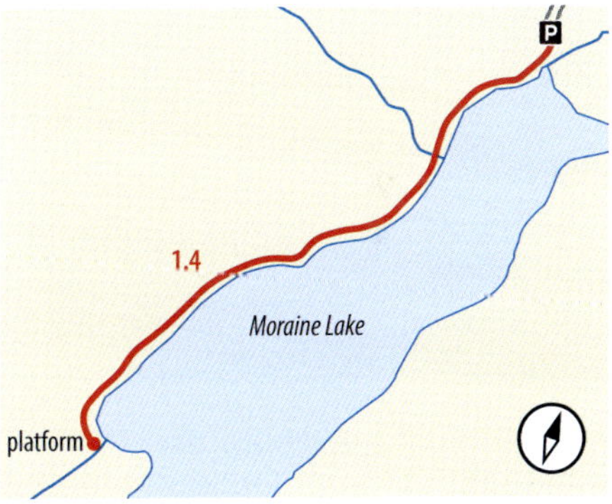

DISTANCE

2.8 km return

ELEVATION GAIN

None

DIFFICULTY

Very easy, recommended for all. Good trail, ending at a platform.

SEASON

Summer and early fall.

OF SPECIAL INTEREST FOR CHILDREN

After the hike, rent a canoe and explore the entire circumference of the lake. Treats are available at Moraine Lake Lodge.

1. The well-signed trail simply follows the lakeshore for 1.4 km to a wooden platform. There are tons of photo opportunities along the way. Take your time and enjoy the ride, but do be respectful of other people and their hiking pace, especially when the trail is busy. Return the same way you came in.

CLOCKWISE FROM TOP LEFT **Moraine Lake, page 71**, Amélie Doucet finds the perfect spot at the lakeshore (photo: Marko Stavric); two minutes from your vehicle sits this amazing view. The water *really is* that colour! ("Why?" ask the kids. "The result of light being refracted by the glacial silt particles suspended in the water," you answer; someone has found a great spot to enjoy the lake (photo: Ruzel Jamilon); paddleboarding is one way to enjoy the lake and the magnificent mountains surrounding it (photo: Mark Koob).

20. ROCKPILE

Picture-perfect views of the lake in less than ten minutes.

LOCATION

Drive west on Highway 1 to Lake Louise and follow the signs to Moraine Lake. Note that the parking lot fills up as early as 6 a.m., even on summer weekdays. On a busy weekend, the shuttle from the Lake Louise overflow is your best bet ($8 each, but price may vary).

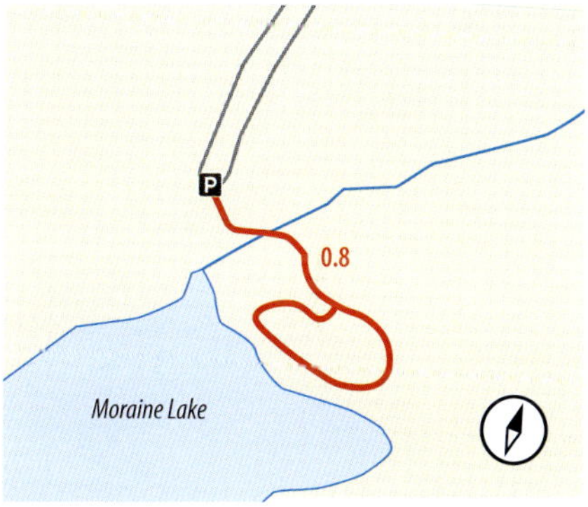

DISTANCE

0.8 km return

ELEVATION GAIN

40 m

DIFFICULTY

Easy, recommended for all. Good trail with some steep steps. Stay on the trail throughout.

SEASON

Summer and early fall.

OF SPECIAL INTEREST FOR CHILDREN

The trail can get very congested. Be patient and respectful of others. Best combined with Moraine Lake and/or Consolation Lakes.

1. From the end of the parking lot the signed trail goes off to the left. Follow the signs up to the Rockpile (turning right a short ways in), explore the area (but stay on the trail), absorb the amazing views (in many directions) and return the same way you came in.

FOLLOWING PAGE, FROM TOP The classic view of the lake from the Rockpile; ascending some well-crafted rock steps, with Tower of Babel in the background (photo: Ruzel Jamilon); Mera, Brianne and Penny Hobbs atop the Rockpile (photo: Matthew Hobbs).

21. CONSOLATION LAKES

A pleasant forest walk to a gem of a lake, surrounded by awe-inspiring, glaciated mountains.

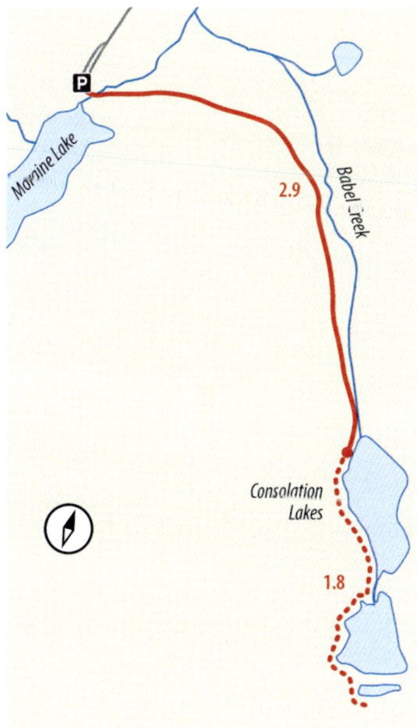

LOCATION

Drive west on Highway 1 to Lake Louise and follow the signs to Moraine Lake. Note that the parking lot fills up as early as 6 a.m., even on summer weekdays. On a busy weekend, the shuttle from the Lake Louise overflow is your best bet ($8 each, but price may vary).

DISTANCE

5.8 km return

ELEVATION GAIN

120 m

DIFFICULTY

Moderate, recommended for children aged 5 and older. Good trail, with some boulder hopping and rocky terrain.

SEASON

Summer and early fall.

OF SPECIAL INTEREST FOR CHILDREN

Boulder-hopping along the lakeshore can be fun for kids. Easily combined with the Rockpile. Check for hiking restrictions (e.g., tight groups of four) due to bears in the area.

1. From the end of the parking lot the signed trail goes off to the left. Follow the trail past the Rockpile turnoff.

2. The trail goes across a boulder field and then into the forest – wonderfully cooling on a hot summer day. Good thing, as the

CLOCKWISE FROM LEFT Kaeli and Brianne work their way through the boulder field just after the Rockpile (photo: Matthew Hobbs); Shawn and Jennifer Benbow at the first lake (photo: Shawn Benbow); the striking towers on the east face of Mount Babel.

trail gains about 120 vertical metres. Along the way there are multiple opportunities to take little side trails to see Babel Creek on the left. Be patient and take one of the trails higher up that is easier and less steep.

3. The trail ends just before the actual lakeshore. Even here the views of awesome Mount Babel (towering over the west side of the lake) and glaciated Quadra Mountain are fantastic.

4. Scrambling over boulders to the lakeshore is the best way to fully experience the lake. Be very careful if you choose to do so, however. Most of the boulders are quite stable, but the odd one will move or shift. There is a faint trail alongside the lake, but it is not recommended. Stay by the lake outlet and cool your feet in the icy water instead. Return the same way you came in.

Going Farther: south end of the Consolation lakes

For advanced hikers who are comfortable negotiating boulder fields and tricky terrain, this extension provides wonderful views throughout.

Distance

Add 3.6 km return

Elevation gain

Minimal

Difficulty

Very strenuous, recommended for children aged 12 and older. There is no trail, and the footing is challenging throughout. Wait until mid-July and don't go if there is snow.

1. Hike carefully around the west side of the two lakes. Go as far as you would like. The far south end of the second lake offers an outstanding view to the north, especially on a clear day. Return the same way you came in. Returning via the east side of the lakes is possible but not recommended, and take into account that this will require you to ford the lake outlet to get back to the main trail.

FROM LEFT The view from the south end of the first lake; the even more impressive view from the south end of the second lake.

22. LARCH VALLEY

Very simply a must-do hike at some point in your life!

LOCATION

Drive west on Highway 1 to Lake Louise and follow the signs to Moraine Lake. Note the parking lot fills up as early as 6 a.m., even on summer weekdays. On a busy weekend, the shuttle from the Lake Louise overflow is your best bet ($8 each, but price may vary).

DISTANCE

8.6 km return

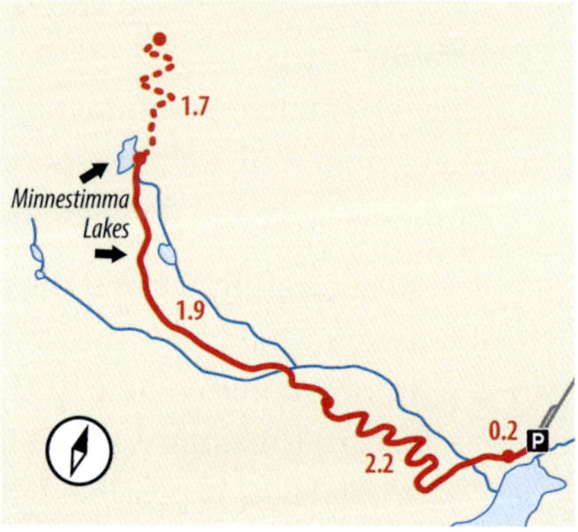

ELEVATION GAIN

540 m; high point: 2425 m

DIFFICULTY

Strenuous, recommended for children aged 6 and older. Excellent trail throughout.

SEASON

Summer and early fall.

OF SPECIAL INTEREST FOR CHILDREN

Obviously a great larch season trip! Check for hiking restrictions (e.g., tight groups of four) due to bears in the area. Can be combined with Eiffel Lake but makes for a very long day.

1. The signed trailhead is at the north end of the parking lot. Follow the trail for 200 m to a signed junction. Turn right onto the Larch Valley/Minnestimma Lakes trail. Remember to check the sign to see if hiking in a tight group of four is recommended or mandatory.

2. Follow the trail for several kilometres up long switchbacks to another junction. Left goes to Eiffel Lake. Stay right and continue up to Larch Valley.

3. Get ready for great views of Eiffel Peak, Pinnacle Mountain and Mount Temple. Turning around allows you to see the

CLOCKWISE FROM TOP One of the most aesthetically beautiful scenes in the Rockies, and Shawn Benbow has captured it perfectly; passing the upper Minnestimma Lake (photo: Shawn Benbow); Sophie Bullock and Noah Koob hike the Larch Valley trail (photo: Tanya Koob).

magnificent Valley of the Ten Peaks. Follow the trail up to the small and shallow Minnestimma Lakes. Either return the same way you came in or continue on to Sentinel Pass.

Going Farther: Sentinel Pass

A steep grind up to a fine viewpoint.

Distance

Add 3.4 km return

Elevation Gain

Add 185 m; high point: 2610 m

Difficulty

Very strenuous, recommended for children aged 10 and older. Good but steep trail throughout.

1. The route is obvious. Follow the trail up several long switchbacks to the pass. You now get a view of the mountains on the north side, Lefroy being one of the more prominent ones. Of course, the view of the Ten Peaks and Minnestimma Lakes is probably going to be the highlight. Return the way same you came in. **Note:** Ascending Mount Temple is *not* a family hike – it's a very serious and difficult scramble for those with a ton of experience.

FROM LEFT The clearly defined zigzag trail up to Sentinel Pass (photo: Shawn Benbow); Noah Koob at the pass, taking in the view over the other side (photo: Tanya Koob).

23. EIFFEL LAKE

A longer and less popular hike than Larch Valley, but with stunning views of the Ten Peaks.

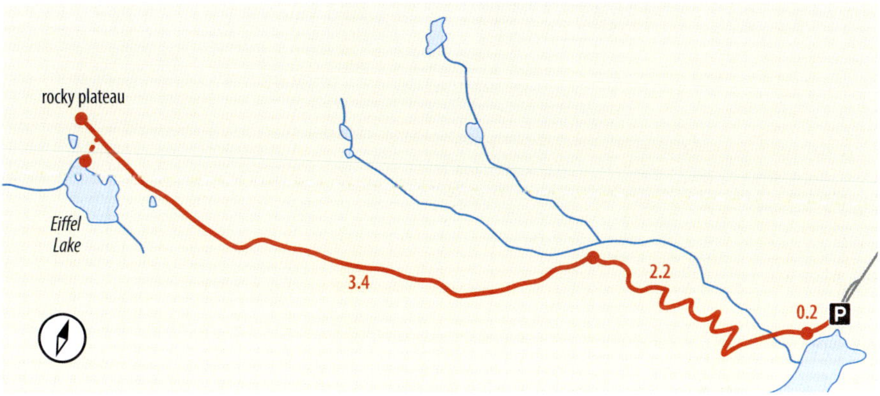

LOCATION

Drive west on Highway 1 to Lake Louise and follow the signs to Moraine Lake. Note the parking lot fills up as early as 6 a.m., even on summer weekdays. On a busy weekend, the shuttle from the Lake Louise overflow is your best bet ($8 each, but price may vary).

DISTANCE

11.6 km return

ELEVATION GAIN

365 m; high point: 2255 m

DIFFICULTY

Strenuous, recommended for children aged 8 and older. Excellent trail throughout.

SEASON

Summer and early fall.

OF SPECIAL INTEREST FOR CHILDREN

Excellent intermediate hike for kids, with a decent amount of elevation gain and fantastic views. Check for hiking restrictions

Sweet views of some of the Ten Peaks accompany Amélie, Kyle and Emily as they hike around Eiffel Peak towards the lake (photo: Marko Stavric).

(e.g., tight groups of four) due to bears in the area. Steep snowbanks often spill across the trail well into the summer. Early-season attempts may be thwarted by snow. This hike can be combined with Larch Valley, but it makes for a very long day.

1. The signed trailhead is at the north end of the parking lot. Follow the trail for 200 m to a signed junction. Turn right onto the Eiffel Lake trail. Remember to check the sign to see if hiking in a tight group of four is recommended or mandatory.
2. Follow the trail for several kilometres up long switchbacks to another junction.
3. Turn left onto the Eiffel Lake trail and follow it around Eiffel Peak, high above the valley. Views improve dramatically throughout.
4. The goal is to hike a short distance past Eiffel Lake to the rocky plateau above it. Have a break and then return the same way you came in. Continuing on to Wenkchemna Pass is an option but makes for an almost 20-km day.

5. Optional: Scrambling down to the lake can be very rewarding, especially on a still day when lake reflections are possible. The best place to do so is about 150 m before the rocky plateau, where a rocky drainage runs down the mountain. There is a faint trail going down to the lake. Carefully descend the steep terrain to the lakeshore. Explore and then return the same way you came in.

FROM TOP The gang arrives at a viewpoint above Eiffel Lake (photo: Marko Stavric); on clear, calm days, the reward of getting down to the shores of Eiffel Lake can be breathtaking lake reflections.

Yoho National Park

YOHO NATIONAL PARK

Stretching the upper limit of driving time for day trips (2.5 hours from Calgary), Yoho offers a number of fantastic hikes suitable for young kids. All amenities and a tourist information centre are available in the town of Field, about 30 km west of Lake Louise.

Unfortunately, the crown jewel of Yoho, Lake O'Hara, is difficult to access, because of the requirement to make reservations months in advance. This is why trips in that area are not described in this book. There are several excellent family hikes in the Lake O'Hara area. Refer to Tony Daffern's *Popular Day Hikes: Canadian Rockies* for descriptions.

The other jewel of Yoho, Emerald Lake, thankfully is quite accessible (although often crowded on most summer weekends) and makes for a wonderful family hike.

Yoho is also home to Takakkaw Falls, the second-highest waterfall in Canada, an attraction that draws hikers and tourists from all corners of the globe. For those considering an extended stay near the falls, there is a walk-in campsite nearby and also a backcountry campsite at Laughing Falls.

Other camping options for the Yoho area include Hoodoo Creek, Kicking Horse and Monarch. Call 1-877-RESERVE for frontcountry campgrounds and 1-250-343-6783 for backcountry ones.

PREVIOUS PAGE The stunning colours of Sherbrooke Lake.

24. PAGET PEAK LOOKOUT

A great workout to an amazing viewpoint.

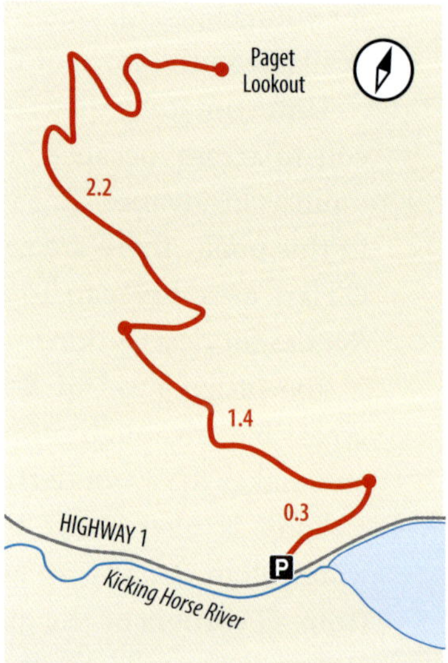

LOCATION

Drive 14.9 km past the Lake Louise turnoff and turn right, into the Sherbrooke Creek parking lot.

DISTANCE

7.8 km return

ELEVATION GAIN

520 m; high point: 2135 m

DIFFICULTY

Strenuous, recommended for children aged 7 and older. Good trail throughout, with rockier terrain higher up.

SEASON

Summer and early fall.

OF SPECIAL INTEREST FOR CHILDREN

A good physical challenge for younger kids. Making it to the lookout can provide good motivation. If things don't look good for the lookout en route, downgrade to Sherbrooke Lake.

1. From the trailhead, go up through the metal gate and then follow the trail for a few hundred metres. Turn left at the signed junction.

2. Continue on this trail for 1.4 km to another signed junction. Turn right, onto the Paget Lookout trail, and hike 2.2 km through forest and up switchbacks to the lookout. Enjoy the terrific views of Wapta Lake far below and glaciated Mount Victoria, as well as other views, and then return the same way you came in. Note that although the summit of Paget Peak is rated as an easy scramble, it is very steep and very loose. This extension is not recommended for families.

CLOCKWISE FROM TOP The trail and good views of Mount Ogden; Noah enjoys a satisfying view to the west (photo: Tanya Koob); Noah and Tanya Koob at the Lookout, with the steep, rocky slopes of Paget Peak behind (photo: Mark Koob).

3. Optional: On return, if energy and motivation are still in abundance, follow the signs to Sherbrooke Lake (see next trip).

25. SHERBROOKE LAKE

A pleasant forest hike to a classic glacier-fed lake.

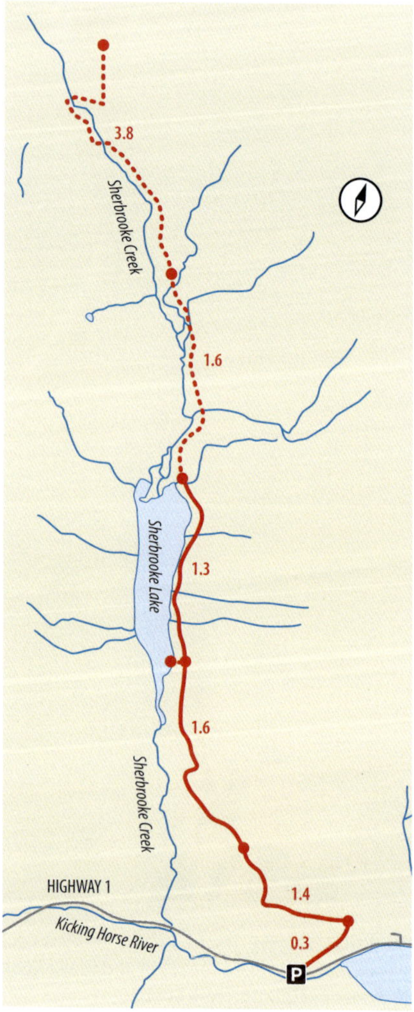

LOCATION

On Highway 1, drive 14.9 km past the Lake Louise turnoff and turn right, into the Sherbrooke Creek parking lot.

DISTANCE

6.6 km return

ELEVATION GAIN

165 m

DIFFICULTY

Moderate, recommended for children aged 5 and older. Good trail all the way, with a few steep sections and lots of tree roots.

SEASON

Summer and fall.

OF SPECIAL INTEREST FOR CHILDREN

A great introduction to more moderate hikes for the kids, without too much elevation gain.

1. From the trailhead, go up through the metal gate and then follow the trail for a few hundred metres. Turn left at the signed junction.
2. Continue on this trail for 1.4 km to another signed junction. Keep going straight and hike 1.6 km to the lake. As you approach the lake, watch for a trail branching off to the left

that goes to the lakeshore within a minute. Views of the lake and Mount Ogden above it are fantastic from this vantage point. Return the same way you came in, or continue the trip to the north end of the lake (highly recommended).

3. Optional: 20 minutes of relatively easy hiking takes you to the north end of the lake. The trail does get a little narrow and exposed near the end. Views are excellent throughout.

Going Farther: North End of the Lake and Beyond

A waterfall and the pleasant meadows above are the draw here.

Distance

Add 2.6–5.8 km return

Elevation Gain

Minimal to the end of the lake; 85 m to the meadows

Difficulty

Easy to the end of the lake, moderately strenuous to the meadow; recommended for children aged 7 and older. Steep trail up to the meadow.

1. Simply follow the trail to the north end of the lake. It does get a little narrow, with a drop-off on the left side near the end.
2. Continue up the valley, as the steep trail starts up the headwall separating Sherbrooke Lake from the meadows above. The highlight of this section is a water cascade near the top. Watch the kids here – the drop-off is quite severe.
3. Eventually the trail emerges onto the open terrain of the valley above. Call it a day here or follow the trail to the north end of the valley. Two stream crossings (on log bridges) and great views make this a worthwhile trek if time and energy permit. Travel beyond the north end of the meadow gets tricky and makes for an extremely long day, and thus not recommended. Return the same way you came in.

CLOCKWISE FROM TOP Sherbrooke Lake on a calm summer morning; across the lake rises Mount Ogden; Kyle Kitagawa crosses the creek in the valley above the lake; beautifully captured view of the cascade. (Middle and both bottom photos: Denise Kitagawa and family.)

Going Farther: Niles Meadow

A “feather in your cap” trip for family hikes. Makes for a very long day but the environs of the meadow are superb.

Distance

Add 7.6 km return

Elevation gain

Add 240 m

Difficulty

Very strenuous, recommended for children aged 12 and older. Good trail most of the way.

1. From the north end of the valley, continue on the trail as it re-enters the forest.
2. The only difficulty occurs when the trail seems to disappear at the side of Sherbrooke Creek. Cross the creek here and find the trail on the other side. Follow it for a few more kilometres into the stunning Niles Meadow. Return the same way you came in.

FROM LEFT Another neat water feature on the way to Niles Meadow; Greg Ng, Maria MacAulay and Amélie Doucet enter Niles Meadow (photo: Marko Stavric).

26. TAKAKKAW FALLS

One of the easiest yet most impressive hikes in the book.

LOCATION

On Highway 1, drive 22 km past the Lake Louise turnoff and turn right, onto Yoho Valley Road. Follow the road for 13 km to the Takakkaw Falls parking lot.

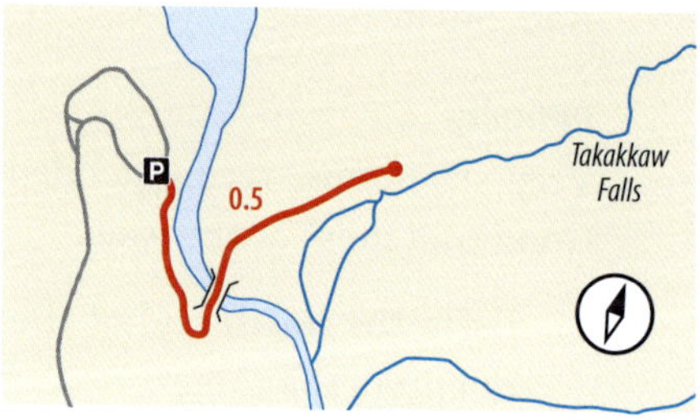

DISTANCE

1 km return

ELEVATION GAIN

Minimal

DIFFICULTY

Very easy, recommended for all. Paved trail all the way, with options to explore primitive trails closer to the falls.

SEASON

Summer and fall.

OF SPECIAL INTEREST FOR CHILDREN

You can get close enough to the falls to feel the spray. The boulders near the stream provide interesting scrambling. The main trail is stroller-friendly.

1. Hike the obvious paved path towards the falls, cross the bridge over the Yoho River and follow the path to its end.
2. There are many primitive trails that can get you closer to the falls, and the boulders by the river are great for exploration, but use discretion and keep an eye on the young ones. Back on the other side of the river, the red Adirondack chairs just south of the bridge make for good photo opportunities.

FROM LEFT The Koobs on the paved trail (photo: Mark Koob); Leah Jones has found a great spot above the trail to get close to the falls (photo: Greg Jones).

27. YOHO LAKE

Escape the crowds and enjoy a rewarding hike to a pristine alpine lake.

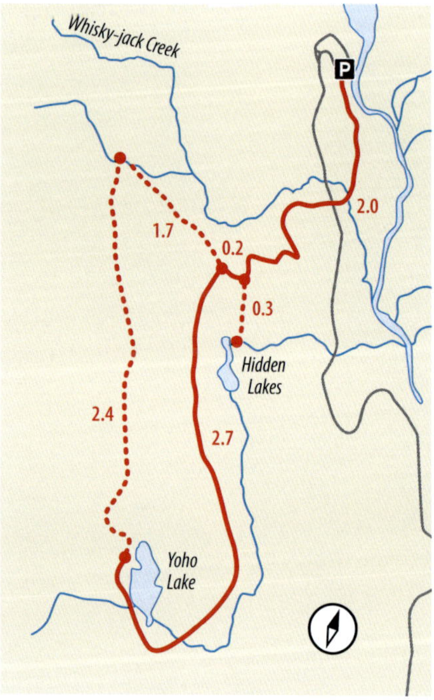

LOCATION

On Highway 1, drive 22 km past the Lake Louise turn-off and turn right, onto Yoho Valley Road. Follow the road for 13 km to the Takakkaw Falls parking lot.

DISTANCE

9.8 km return

ELEVATION GAIN

290 m

DIFFICULTY

Strenuous, recommended for children aged 7 and older. Good trail all the way.

SEASON

Summer and early fall.

OF SPECIAL INTEREST FOR CHILDREN

Recommended for older kids who are used to long forest walks and fairly steep sections of trail. The kids will probably enjoy the lake and the Going Farther option even more.

1. From the parking lot, hike towards Takakkaw Falls but do not cross the bridge. Hike past the Adirondack chairs and follow the connector trail that soon crosses the road and leads to the Whiskey Jack Hostel. The signed trailhead is reached just before the hostel. Note that this point is considered to be the Takakkaw Falls parking lot, in reference to the distances on the signs.

Easy walking and good views to start the trip.

2. Hike 1.1 km to the first junction. A big chunk of the elevation is gained here and there are occasional good views of Takakkaw Falls.
3. At the first junction, a side trip to the two Hidden Lakes is optional (600 m return). The second lake is quite pretty, though no one is about to be "blown out of the water"!
4. From the first junction, another 200 m takes you to the second. Go straight.
5. About 2.7 km of generally easy hiking takes you to Yoho Lake. There are numerous points along the west shore to get good views. Hike past the campground to the red Adirondack chairs on the northwest side of the lake for the best views. Return the same way you came in, or make a loop of it as described below (highly recommended).

Going Farther: The Loop via Highline Trail

Amazing open views for the small price of some additional elevation gain and a little extra distance.

Distance

Add an additional 1.5 km to the return trip

FROM LEFT Decent views of Michael Peak from the south end of Yoho Lake; Wapta Mountain towering above Yoho Lake.

Elevation Gain

Add 135 m

Difficulty

Strenuous, recommended for children aged 8 and older. Good trail most of the way, with a few rocky sections.

1. Go to the Yoho Lake campground and find the food hanger. From there, hike the trail that goes north. Follow it for 2.4 km to the next junction. Once above the treeline, the views to the east over Waputik Icefield are outstanding.
2. At the junction, turn right and follow the signs back to the Takakkaw Falls parking lot.

On the Highline trail just before the view really starts to open up.

28. ICELINE TRAIL

A tough but thrilling hike to the stunning and barren environs of Emerald Glacier.

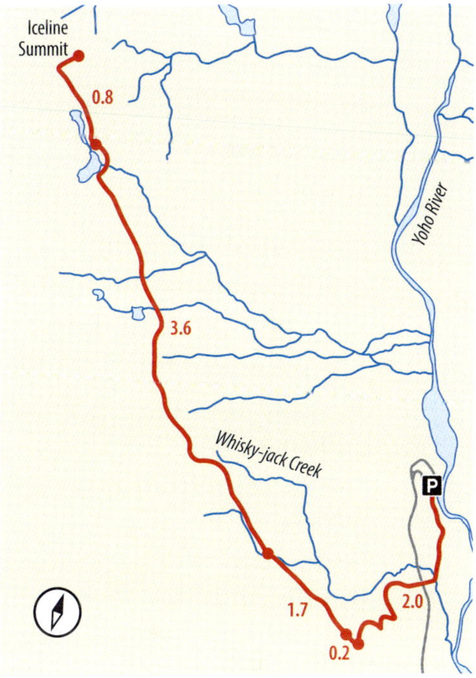

LOCATION

On Highway 1, drive 22 km past the Lake Louise turn-off and turn right, onto Yoho Valley Road. Follow the road for 13 km to the Takakkaw Falls parking lot.

DISTANCE

14.6 km return

ELEVATION GAIN

685 m; high point: 2210 m

DIFFICULTY

Very strenuous, recommended for children aged 12 and older. Steep, rocky trail once above the treeline, with a few narrow sections.

SEASON

Mid-July to early fall.

OF SPECIAL INTEREST FOR CHILDREN

Perhaps the kids' first close-up look at a glacier. Lots of room for exploration.

1. From the parking lot, hike towards Takakkaw Falls but do not cross the bridge. Hike past the Adirondack chairs and follow the connector trail that soon crosses the road and leads to the Whiskey Jack Hostel. The signed trailhead is reached just before the hostel. Note that this point is considered to be the Takakkaw Falls parking lot, in reference to the distances on the signs.

2. Hike 1.1 km to the first junction. A big chunk of the elevation is gained here, and there are occasional good views of Takakkaw Falls.
3. At the first junction, a side trip to the two Hidden Lakes is optional (600 m return). The second lake is quite pretty, though again no one is about to be "blown out of the water"!
4. From the first junction, another 200 m takes you to the second. Turn right towards Iceline Trail.
5. Hike 1.7 km to the next junction and take the right fork, as signed.
6. It's about 3.6 km, across the wild moraines below what's left of Emerald Glacier, to the next signed junction. The kids will probably enjoy hopping over the numerous small streams running down from the glacier.
7. The junction sits by two beautiful glacial tarns – one of the big highlights of the trip. Keep going straight, past the tarns, and then turn right, up to the obvious high point, commonly referred to as the Iceline Summit. It's about 800 m from the junction to the summit. Return the same way you came in. From the tarns, there is the option is visit Celeste Lake and then return via Laughing Falls. This option makes for a 19-plus-km day and is not recommended as a family hike.

FACING PAGE, CLOCKWISE FROM TOP Once you get above the treeline, views to the east and northeast are stunning; lots of streams running down from the receding glacier; passing the third tarn and heading to the Iceline Summit in the centre; sometimes, following the trail just means walking across smooth slabs of glacially eroded rock. (All photos: Denise Kitagawa and family.)

29. LAUGHING FALLS

A somewhat dull approach, but the impressive destination makes it worthwhile. A good candidate for a first backcountry camping trip.

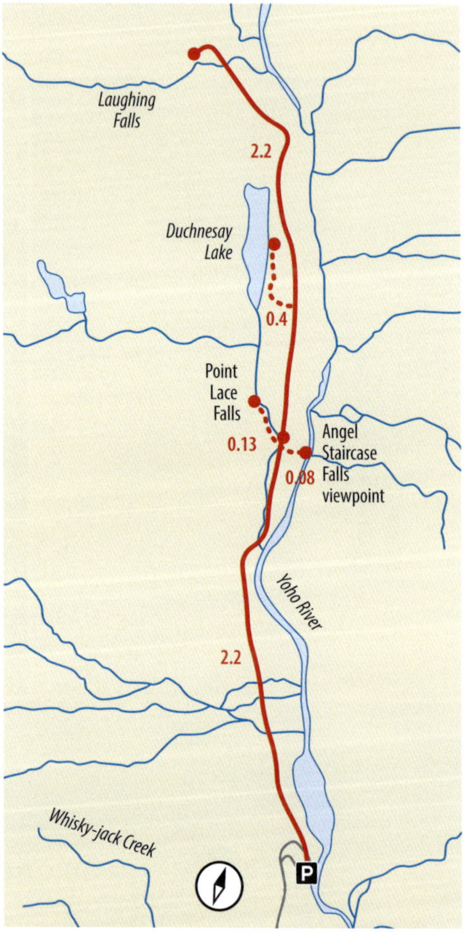

LOCATION

On Highway 1, drive 22 km past the Lake Louise turn-off and turn right, onto Yoho Valley Road. Follow the road for 13 km to the Takakkaw Falls parking lot.

DISTANCE

8.8 km return

ELEVATION GAIN

130 m

DIFFICULTY

Moderate, recommended for children aged 6 and older. Good trail all the way, with one lengthy section of steep uphill.

SEASON

Summer and fall.

OF SPECIAL INTEREST FOR CHILDREN

Lots of great water scenery, especially if you complete the side trips.

1. From the parking lot, hike north on the paved trail for about 500 m, past the Takakkaw Falls campground to the signed trailhead.

FROM LEFT Matt Hobbs has his hands full on the Laughing Falls trail (photo: Brianne Hobbs); Tanya and Noah Koob at the falls (photo: Mark Koob).

2. About 1.7 km of easy trail takes you to the first intersection. Angel's Staircase Falls viewpoint is about 80 m along the trail to the right. Point Lace Falls viewpoint is about 130 m on the trail to the left. Both viewpoints are easy to reach and recommended at this point or on return.

3. The next 2.2 km to Laughing Falls involves a steep climb and then a gradual descent back down to the river. As you approach the falls, there are a few points where you can get close to the always-raging river. Be very careful if you choose to do so, as a slip into the fast-flowing river would probably be fatal.

4. After crossing the Little Yoho River on a bridge, the Laughing Falls campground is reached, with Laughing Falls only a minute upstream. The trail does get close enough to the falls for the kids to get wet from the spray. Don't go beyond this point. Return the same way you came in. Note the 400-m detour to see Duchesnay Lake if you want a little extra exercise and a decent view of an interesting lake.

30. EMERALD LAKE

A wonderful hike around a superbly colourful lake.
One of the many true gems of Yoho.

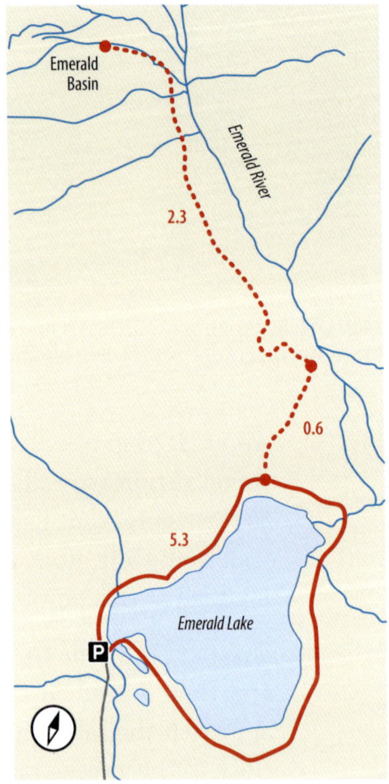

LOCATION

From Highway 1, 1.6 km west of the Field turnoff, take the turnoff to Emerald Lake and follow the road to the parking lot.

DISTANCE

5.3-km loop

ELEVATION GAIN

Minimal

DIFFICULTY

Easy, recommended for all. Excellent semi-paved trail for much of the loop; good mud-packed trail for the rest.

SEASON

Late spring, summer and early fall.

OF SPECIAL INTEREST FOR CHILDREN

After the hike, rent a canoe to explore the lake. Stop at the geologically interesting Natural Bridge when driving back along the approach road. Get there early to beat the crowds.

1. Hike down towards the lake and find the wide, paved trail that starts going around it in a clockwise direction. While the trail isn't right on the lakeshore throughout, there are many spots to enjoy great views of the lake, as well as to take breaks if necessary. Along the north shore there are several minor trails that take you right to the lake, with excellent views of the entire area.

FROM LEFT The Benbow family at the lake whose name so well suits its vivid colour (photo: Shawn Benbow); humans aren't the only life form to enjoy the beauty of the lake.

2. Stay to the right throughout the loop, ignoring the horse trails and other turnoffs, unless you plan to tackle Emerald Basin (see **Going Farther**). Approaching the end of the 5.3-km loop an intersection is reached. Left goes directly to the parking lot and right goes through the Emerald Lake Lodge area. With kids in tow, right may be your best bet! Snacks and beverages are available.

Going Farther: Emerald Basin

A far more intense affair than the Emerald Lake loop, this gets you up to a stunning alpine basin with two waterfalls. This hike definitely favours a bluebird day. A great trail but relentlessly steep for several sections.

Distance

Add 5.8–6.8 km return

Elevation Gain

Add 225 m; high point: 1540 m

Difficulty

Very strenuous, recommended for children aged 12 and older. Good trail most of the way, with a few steep sections and rocky terrain near the waterfalls.

1. The signed turnoff is 2.1 km from the start of the Emerald Lake trail (in a clockwise direction). Turn left onto it and hike 600 m to another sign.
2. Turn left onto the new trail and follow it 2.3 km to the basin. On a clear day, the views of sections of the President Range are incredible.
3. Optional: For those who are comfortable on loose, rocky terrain without a trail, it's possible to hike right up to the obvious dual waterfalls towards the left side of the basin. Return the same way you came in.

CLOCKWISE FROM TOP Spectacular Emerald Basin, with its dual waterfalls at the left; the Natural Bridge; getting up close to the left-hand waterfall.

31. WAPTA FALLS

A long drive but a short hike to an amazing waterfall.

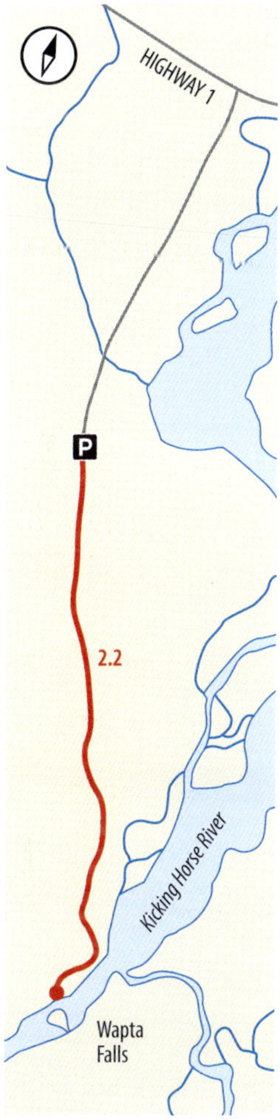

LOCATION

Drive west on Highway 1, past Lake Louise and Field. Look for the turnoff to the Chancellor Peak campground but don't turn there. Drive about 900 m past the campground turnoff and turn left onto an unsigned gravel road. Drive the gravel road 1.7 km to the trailhead.

DISTANCE

1.8 km return

ELEVATION LOSS/GAIN

60 m

DIFFICULTY

Moderate, recommended for children aged 4 and older. Good trail all the way to the falls. Opportunity for off-trail exploration around the falls.

SEASON

Late spring, summer and early fall.

OF SPECIAL INTEREST FOR CHILDREN

Take a raincoat if you want to get close to the falls. The kids will probably want to climb the "hills" in front of the falls – use discretion if you let them. Given the lengthy driving time (approximately 2.75 hours from Calgary), this is best combined with another trip, such as Emerald Lake, or as a stop-off on the way to Golden.

1. Hike the easy, relatively flat trail for about 1.5 km. The trail then gently ascends to a fenced viewpoint above the falls. Note the two "hills" by the falls that offer close-up views.

2. From the first viewpoint, descend the trail, taking a left turn almost right away and arriving at another viewpoint in short order. Going straight at the aforementioned intersection leads to the falls eventually but misses another viewpoint. This route is not as steep as the left-turn route.

3. Continue down to the falls. There is lots of room to explore this area and take in the terrific views. Note the following:
   - Expect to get drenched from the spray if you get close to the falls. Leave all electronic devices a good distance away.
   - The terrain around the falls can be very slippery, steep and dangerous. Proceed with extreme caution.
   - The second "hill" provides an excellent viewpoint but is very slippery to ascend and descend.
   - A small sandy area a short distance downstream is a great place for lunch.

4. Return the same way you came in. Taking the less steep trail is an option here.

CLOCKWISE FROM TOP LEFT Looking down at the falls from one of the upper viewpoints – winter trips here are quite possible and very scenic; Shawn and Jennifer Benbow enjoy the winter view (both upper photos: Shawn Benbow); the falls are spectacular in the summer too (photo: Ruzel Jamilon).

Icefields Parkway (Highway 93 North)

ICEFIELDS PARKWAY (HIGHWAY 93 NORTH)

Let's go camping! Described as one of the most scenic drives in the world, the stretch of highway between Lake Louise and Jasper is not to be missed. And given the lengthy driving time from any major centre, the best and most logical way to experience the parkway is to spend a night or two or three at one of the many campgrounds along the way: Mosquito Creek, Silverhorn Creek and Waterfowl Lake for the southern section; Rampart Creek, Wilcox Creek, Columbia Icefields, Jonas Creek, Honeymoon Lakes, Mount Kerkeslin, Pocahontas, Wabasso and Wapiti for the northern section – book online and book early!

This volume of *Family Walks and Hikes* includes two trips on the southern half of the highway, which can be reached in about 2.5 hours from Calgary, and five trips on the northern half, each necessitating a drive time of about 3.5–4.5 hours one way. If the kids are getting restless during the drive, the parkway offers numerous scenic stops along the way for everyone to stretch their legs. These include Herbert Lake, Crowfoot Glacier, Bow Lake, Waterfowl Lakes and Tangle Falls.

There are no amenities on the southern half of Highway 93 North. Stop at Lake Louise if needed. Saskatchewan River Crossing, halfway between Lake Louise and Jasper, offers lodging, food and gas. The town of Jasper offers all amenities.

PREVIOUS PAGE A family of five enjoys one of the premier views in all of the Rockies from Wilcox Ridge.

CLOCKWISE FROM TOP **Peyto Lake Viewpoints, page 116**, Noah Koob, 8, drinks in the view from near the upper viewpoint (photo: Tanya Koob); **Bow Lake and Falls, page 113**, getting up close to Bow Glacier Falls; **Peyto Lake Viewpoints, page 116**, the rock pile by the lake grants terrific views.

32. HELEN LAKE

Strenuous but superb hike to a beautiful alpine lake amid stunning mountain scenery.

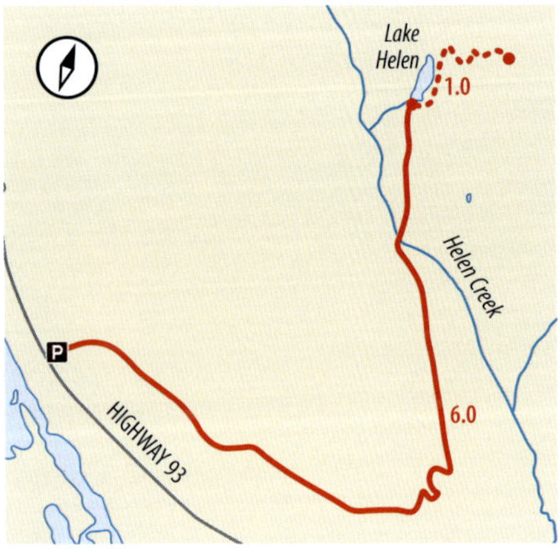

LOCATION

Drive west on Highway 1, past Lake Louise, and take the Highway 93 turnoff (Exit 7) towards Jasper. Drive about 33 km and turn right, into the Helen Lake parking lot.

DISTANCE

12 km return

ELEVATION GAIN

455 m

DIFFICULTY

Strenuous, recommended for children aged 8 and older. Good trail, but tree roots and rocks throughout.

SEASON

Summer and fall.

OF SPECIAL INTEREST FOR CHILDREN

Good chance to see hoary marmots in addition to the lake. Great in late July and early August, when the wildflowers are out.

1. From the trailhead, simply follow the Helen Lake trail for 6 km to the lake. A few of the side trails offer decent views over Bow Lake but are not necessary to visit. Once the trail swings around the hillside, views improve dramatically and get even better as you make your way up the valley. Note the signs urging all to stay on the designated trails. Enjoy the lake and then either return the same way you came in or complete the highly recommended extension.

CLOCKWISE FROM TOP LEFT Early morning mist doesn't always fill the valley, but it's cool when it does; Raff the mountaineer approaches a scenic creek crossing before the lake; Helen Lake is wonderfully backdropped by Cirque Peak, a terrific scramble for when the kids are grown up.

Going Farther: Helen Ridge

Amazing views everyone will want to experience.

Distance

Add 2 km return

Elevation Gain

Add 120 m; high point: 2520 m

Difficulty

Very strenuous, recommended for children aged 10 and older. Good trail, quite steep in places.

1. Follow the obvious trail around the east side of Helen Lake and then up to the ridge above the lake. As expected, views of the surrounding area are spectacular. Return the same way you came in.

FROM TOP Don't forget to turn around as you hike the east shore of the lake; the fascinating rock-folding on the southeast face of Cirque Peak is one of many scenic rewards for making it to the ridge; the view from the ridge now includes glaciated Crowfoot Mountain.

33. BOW LAKE AND FALLS

One of the most beautiful lakes in the Rockies – period! And you get to see a stunning waterfall too.

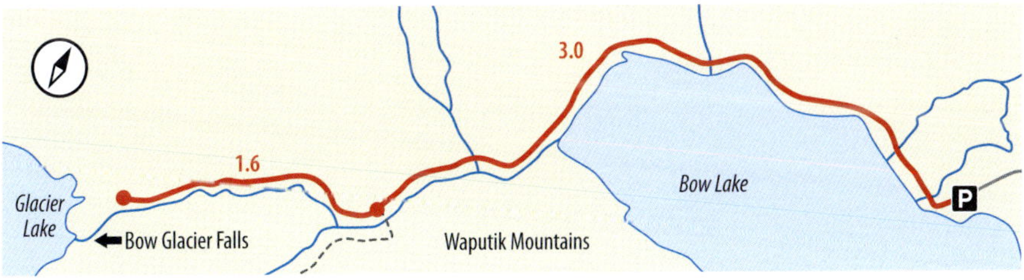

LOCATION

Drive west on Highway 1, past Lake Louise, and take the Highway 93 turnoff (Exit 7) towards Jasper. Drive about 36 km and turn left into the Bow Lake (Num-Ti-Jah Lodge) parking lot.

DISTANCE

9.2 km return

ELEVATION GAIN

135 m; high point: 2080 m

DIFFICULTY

Moderately difficult, recommended for children aged 7 and older; varied terrain underfoot: mud trail, some tree roots in one section, steep stairs, and rocky terrain before the falls. Expect to do a little boulder-hopping too.

SEASON

Summer and early fall.

OF SPECIAL INTEREST FOR CHILDREN

Even the simple hike around the northwest side of Bow Lake makes for a worthwhile trip, especially on a clear, calm day. Kids will love the colour of the lake. Early morning trips are preferable for lake reflections, and morning to early afternoon for the best light.

CLOCKWISE FROM TOP LEFT Winter at Bow Lake can be a blast and incredibly scenic; Sophie Bullock and her mum, Joyce Cortes, at the remarkable Bow Glacier Falls (photo: Tanya Koob); Bow Lake is one of the Rockies' prettiest; the hike out can be incredibly scenic as well.

A busier Bow Lake later in the day. The bridge at left is a favourite place for photos and kids.

1. Hike past Num-Ti-Jah Lodge and find the signed Bow Glacier Falls trail at the west end of a parking area for guests of the lodge. Before doing that, though, you may wish to explore the worthwhile trail at the end of the parking lot on the left (south) side, which goes directly to the lakeshore for some outstanding views and scenery. You may have to return to the parking lot to then find the start of the main trail, past the lodge.
2. Once on the Bow Glacier Falls trail, hike for 3 km, around the lake, over two sets of gravel flats and up the right side of a deep canyon. This section is quite steep, and there are sections where a slip down the left side would be very bad. Hang on to the young ones.
3. After the canyon section, you soon reach a sign for the Alpine Club of Canada's Bow Hut. Keep going straight, eventually arriving at the hanging valley where Bow Glacier Falls sits.
4. Descend into the valley and hike on rockier terrain to the base of the falls. There is much terrain to explore around the base of the falls if desired. Thankfully, most of the rock does not get slippery when wet, but extreme caution is still required if you choose to let the kids scramble up to higher terrain near the waterfall. Return the same way you came in.

34. PEYTO LAKE VIEWPOINTS

A super-easy and short interpretive walk to a magnificent view of colourful Peyto Lake.

LOCATION

Drive west on Highway 1, past Lake Louise, and take the Highway 93 turnoff (Exit 7) towards Jasper. Drive about 41 km and turn left into the Bow Summit parking lot.

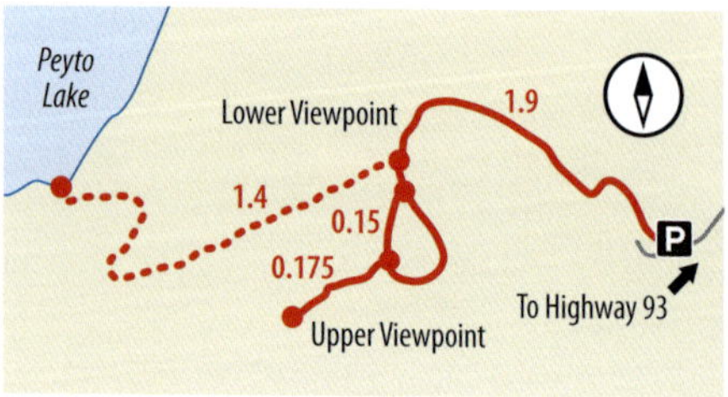

DISTANCE

1.9 km return

ELEVATION GAIN

50 m

DIFFICULTY

Easy, recommended for all; paved trail.

SEASON

Summer and early fall.

OF SPECIAL INTEREST FOR CHILDREN

Combine this trip with 35. Bow Summit Lookout Site (next) for great views of both lakes. The lower viewpoint is usually very crowded, the upper viewpoint less so.

1. The paved trail starts at the north end of the parking lot and is easy to follow. Stop to read the interpretive information panels along the way. Follow the trail for about 500 m to the potentially very crowded lower viewing platform and a wonderful view of the turquoise waters of Peyto Lake.

CLOCKWISE FROM TOP What a view only ten minutes from the parking lot – some think the lake is shaped like a ghost, some a dog – ask your kids what they think; a couple at the upper viewpoint looks out towards the magnificent Wapta Icefield; Gavin Emanuel, 3, takes in the view from the upper viewpoint (photo: Katy Emanuel).

2. Continue following the paved trail, soon reaching a three-way junction and an "Explore" sign. This is the beginning of the interpretive loop as well as the gateway to the Bow Summit hike. Take the right fork and hike about 150 m to the first interpretive panel. Look for an unsigned, unpaved trail branching off to the right. Follow this trail for about 175 m (at first ascending and then descending) to the rocky upper viewpoint. As well as enjoying another magnificent and slightly better view of Peyto Lake, you may even get to enjoy some solitude here!

3. Return to the paved trail and continue along the counter-clockwise interpretive loop, eventually retuning to the "Explore" sign. Note that you will encounter signs for the Bow Summit Lookout trail and the trailhead along the loop. If you would like to extend your day, see **35. Bow Summit Lookout Site** (next trip). Otherwise, return to the parking lot the same way you came in or consider another trip extension that takes you closer to Peyto Lake (see **Going Farther: Down to Peyto Lake**, just next).

Going Farther: Down to Peyto Lake

Be one of the few hardy souls to venture all the way down to the shores of the lake. Gaining all that elevation back is the crux of the trip!

Distance

Add 2.8 km return

Elevation loss/gain

Add 260 m

Difficulty

Strenuous, recommended for children aged 10 and older.

1. From the lower viewpoint, continue along the paved trail for a short distance, looking for the trail heading down on the right side.

Five hearty souls enjoy the lakeshore.

2. Follow this steep trail all the way down to the lake, first through forest and then down an avalanche slope.
3. Explore the shores of the lake as desired and then slowly grind your way back up to the viewpoint. Return the way you came in.

35. BOW SUMMIT LOOKOUT SITE

To complement the great view of Peyto Lake, continue up to this former lookout site for an equally enthralling view of Bow Lake.

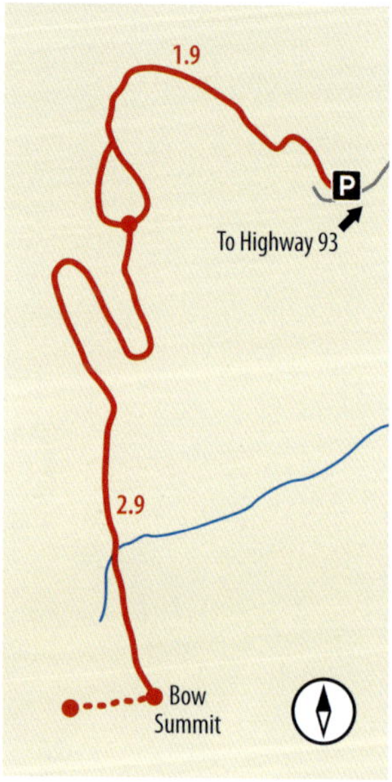

LOCATION

Drive west on Highway 1, past Lake Louise, and take the Highway 93 turnoff (Exit 7) towards Jasper. Drive about 41 km and turn left into the Bow Summit parking lot.

DISTANCE

7.4 km return

ELEVATION GAIN

245 m; high point: 2315 m

DIFFICULTY

Moderate, recommended for children aged 6 and older; good, gently graded trail throughout.

SEASON

Summer and early fall.

OF SPECIAL INTEREST FOR CHILDREN

Most people, families included, take on this hike in conjunction with Peyto Lake Viewpoints. Note that the trail is chariot/jogging-stroller friendly when dry.

1. Follow the instructions for 34. Peyto Lake Viewpoints. You will find the trailhead to Bow Summit a short distance around the loop trail, a few hundred metres past the turnoff to the upper viewpoint, assuming you have hiked the loop in a counter-clockwise direction

FROM TOP The view of Bow Lake and the surrounding mountains is the feature highlight of this trip; entering the superb environs around Bow Summit.

The scramblers' option to reach the rock face above.

2. From the trail sign, follow the wide trail for 2.9 km to a small, elevated open area with an awesome view of Bow Lake. Return the way you came in or continue with an added scramble in step 3.
3. For the budding scrambler, follow the very steep scree trail from the open area up to the rock face above. The view is only slightly better, but undertake this scramble for the exercise and feeling of accomplishment for the kids. However, this section is only for kids who are comfortable on steep, loose scree.

FROM TOP **Bow Lake and Falls, page 113**, perfect lake reflections often occur early in the morning; **Bow Summit Lookout Site, page 120**, at elevations around 2300 m, snow often persists into July.

36. MISTAYA CANYON

Short, easy hike down to a remarkable water-eroded canyon.

LOCATION

Drive west on Highway 1, past Lake Louise, and take the Highway 93 turnoff (Exit 7) towards Jasper. Drive about 70 km and turn left into the Mistaya Canyon parking lot.

DISTANCE

0.6 km return

ELEVATION LOSS/GAIN

60 m

DIFFICULTY

Very easy, recommended for all. A good trail down to the canyon. Off-trail travel at the shore of the river.

SEASON

Late spring, summer and fall.

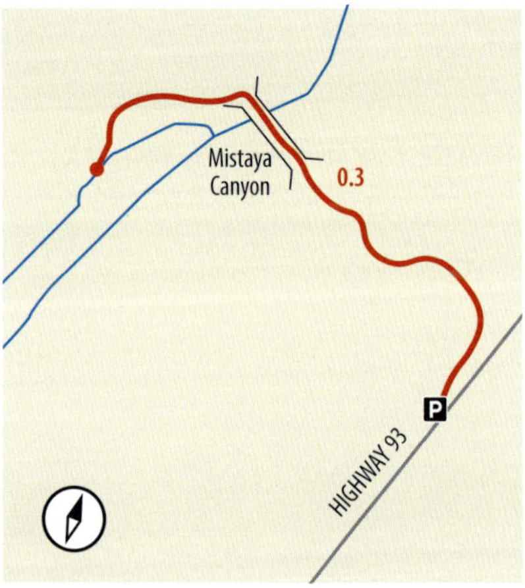

OF SPECIAL INTEREST FOR CHILDREN

Short, easy and spectacular. Watch the kids carefully if you choose to go down to the Mistaya River.

1. From the trailhead, hike about 300 m down to the bridge over the canyon and enjoy the views from the bridge. Pre-warn the kids about the dangers of falling into the canyon, and hold hands if need be.

2. Optional: Follow the trail on the other side of the bridge that goes down to the mighty Mistaya River. Be *very* careful about getting too close to the edge. There is flat, stable rock a short ways upstream where the kids can enjoy the rushing water.

FOLLOWING PAGE, CLOCKWISE FROM TOP The canyon (photo: Ruzel Jamilon); the rock on the west side of the river provides a great viewpoint – just don't get too close; looking down the canyon from the west side.

37. PARKER RIDGE

A relatively short hike to a fabulous viewpoint overlooking the mighty Saskatchewan Glacier.

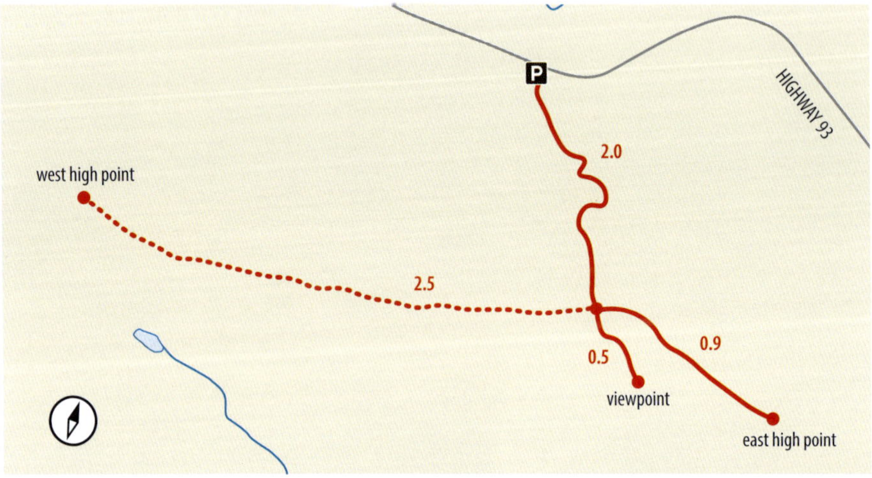

LOCATION

Drive west on Highway 1, past Lake Louise, and take the Highway 93 turnoff (Exit 7) towards Jasper. Drive about 117 km and turn left into the Parker Ridge parking lot.

DISTANCE

5.8–6.8 km return

ELEVATION GAIN

320 m; high point: 2320 m

DIFFICULTY

Moderate, recommended for children aged 5 and older. Good trail all the way (stay on it throughout to avoid damaging the fragile environment).

SEASON

Summer and early fall (snow patches may persist well into July).

ABOVE, FROM LEFT Brianne with baby, dad Matt, Crux the dog and Grandma (Pat Hobbs) on this wonderful trail, with Mount Athabasca a constant companion (photo: Gordon Hobbs); Nicole Lisafeld checks out Saskatchewan Glacier and Castleguard Mountain. **BELOW** The Hobbs clan approaches the east summit (photo: Matthew Hobbs).

OF SPECIAL INTEREST FOR CHILDREN

Great views requiring minimal effort. Let the kids know why it's important to stay on the trail in this fragile area. Note that this trail is prone to closure in late spring in order to protect the delicate environment.

1. From the signed trailhead, follow the well-trodden trail up through several switchbacks to the ridge, about 2 km from the start.
2. From the ridge, you can descend a short distance (about 500 m) down the other side for terrific views of the Saskatchewan Glacier and/or continue following a minor trail as it veers left (east) towards the obvious east high point about 900 m away. Return the same way you came in, or do the extension to the west high point.

FROM LEFT The extension to the west High Point is the lighter-coloured rock below awe-inspiring Mount Athabasca (photo: Shawn Benbow); early-season attempts often require detours to get around huge snowbanks.

Going Farther: West High Point

For even better views and extra exercise.

Distance

Add 5 km return

Elevation Gain

Add 200–320 m; high point: 2600 m

Difficulty

Strenuous, recommended for children aged 7 and older. Faint trail and off-trail travel to the high point.

1. From the east high point, start by returning the way you came and simply continue going west towards the other obvious high point along the ridge.
2. It's up to you how far you go. The farthest point would be the significant summit about 2.5 km from the low point. It gets fairly steep towards the top. This summit is for experienced families only. After enjoying another magnificent view, return the same way you came in.

38. WILCOX PASS

The big brother of Parker Ridge. Outrageously stunning views of the Athabasca Glacier and mountains of the Columbia Icefield. Another must-do route.

LOCATION

Drive west on Highway 1, past Lake Louise, and take the Highway 93 turnoff (Exit 7) towards Jasper. Drive about 123 km and turn right, into the Wilcox Creek campground. Park at the trailhead kiosk, a short distance up the road.

DISTANCE

6.8 km return

ELEVATION GAIN

320 m; high point: 2375 m

DIFFICULTY

Strenuous, recommended for children aged 6 and older. Good trail throughout, with a few steep sections.

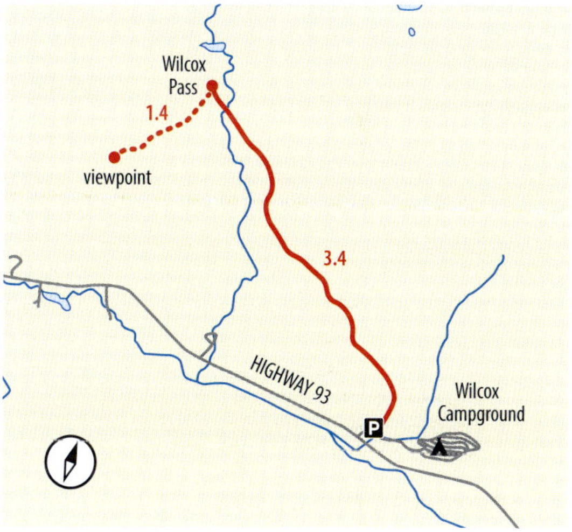

SEASON

Midsummer and early fall (snow patches may persist well into July).

OF SPECIAL INTEREST FOR CHILDREN

Perhaps the kids' first experience seeing heavily glaciated mountains.

1. Hike the steep trail through forest and on a short boardwalk eventually out onto an open ridge.
2. Continue in a northwest direction, enjoying the increasingly terrific view to the west. Ignore the side trails. The pass is

CLOCKWISE FROM TOP The Adirondack chairs provide a perfect viewpoint and rest stop for Brianne and Mera Hobbs (photo: Matthew Hobbs); mother and son before one of the premier views in the Rockies (photo: Mark Koob); Noah Koob leads his dad, Mark, up the trail (photo: Tanya Koob).

marked with a sign. Return the same way you came in, or complete the highly recommended traverse over to Wilcox Ridge.

Going Farther: Wilcox Ridge

The "must-do" part of a must-do route.

Distance

Add 2.8 km return

Elevation Gain

Add 100 m; high point: 2420 m

Difficulty

Strenuous, recommended for children aged 6 and older. Good trail, but several short steep sections.

1. Simply follow the well-marked trail up and over a few bumps to one of the finest viewpoints in the Rockies. Drink up the awe-inspiring views and then return the same way you came in.

TOP TO BOTTOM The trail is easy to follow; mounts Athabasca and Andromeda and the rapidly receding Athabasca Glacier are the highlights of the view.

39. FOREFIELD TRAIL / TOE OF ATHABASCA GLACIER

Two short hikes that can be combined for a terrific overview of the Columbia Icefields area.

LOCATION

Drive west on Highway 1, past Lake Louise, and take the Highway 93 turnoff (Exit 7) towards Jasper. Drive about 126 km and turn left into the Athabasca Glacier parking lot. Park in either the Forefield parking lot (described below) or the Toe of the Glacier parking lot.

DISTANCE

5.4 km return

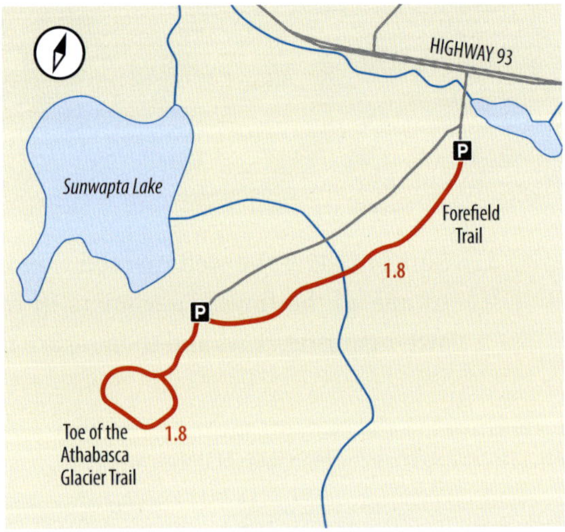

ELEVATION GAIN

50 m

DIFFICULTY

Easy, recommended for children aged 5 and older. Rocky trail and a few steep sections.

SEASON

Late spring, summer and early fall.

OF SPECIAL INTEREST FOR CHILDREN

Note: These trails can also be done individually. Perhaps someone can convince mum or dad to retrieve the car from the Forefield parking lot and drive down to the Toe of the Glacier parking lot to pick everyone up!

1. From the Forefield parking lot (recommended because it sports a glorious view of Mount Athabasca, whereas the Toe of the Glacier parking lot does not), hike the wide, paved trail west. The trail soon shrinks to a rocky, narrow, single-track trail.

2. Follow the trail as it winds through the rocky terrain, over a stream (log bridge) and then gradually descends to the Toe of the Glacier parking lot. Take your time and enjoy the changing views and amazing glacier scenery.
3. Optional and highly recommended: Hike the well-marked and signed Toe of the Glacier trail for excellent views of the Athabasca Glacier. For everyone's safety, stick to the trail and don't

TOP TO BOTTOM Brianne, Penny and Mera Hobbs near the beginning of the hike; Penny and Mera Hobbs at the 1992 marker; the Hobbs sisters at the end of the hike, with the still mighty though now receding Athabasca Glacier behind them. (All three photos: Matthew Hobbs.)

40. TANGLE FALLS

Not really a full-length hike, but a great place to stop and take in a scenic roadside waterfall, with the option to explore the multi-tiered fall

Note: Since all you have to do to begin this route is cross the road you arrived on, a map didn't seem necessary.

LOCATION

Drive west on Highway 1, past Lake Louise, and take the Highway 93 turnoff (Exit 7) towards Jasper. Drive about 133 km to the signed parking lot (7.5 km past Columbia Icefield Centre). Be very careful crossing the road to the waterfall.

DISTANCE

Minimal, 0.4 km return

ELEVATION GAIN

Minimal, 35 m

DIFFICULTY

Easy, recommended for children of all ages, but watch the young ones carefully; also watch your footing around the falls, as the terrain can be slippery.

SEASON

Summer and early fall

OF SPECIAL INTEREST FOR CHILDREN

You can get right up to the falls and there is lots of room to explore.

1. Carefully cross the road and you are there. Most will want to explore the falls on either side. There are multiple tiers to check out. Watch the kids carefully here.

CLOCKWISE FROM TOP The roadside view of the falls; the magic of long-exposure photography; the Benbow family at the upper tier. (All three photos: Shawn Benbow.)

41. BEAUTY CREEK

If the drive is getting long, this is a great little trip to stretch your legs and take in some fine water scenery.

LOCATION

Drive west on Highway 1, past Lake Louise, and take the Highway 93 turnoff (Exit 7) towards Jasper. Drive about 126 km to the Columbia Icefield Centre and zero your odometer. The trailhead is about 15.5 km farther north along Highway 93. Turn right into a small parking area. If you get to the Beauty Creek Hostel you have gone too far.

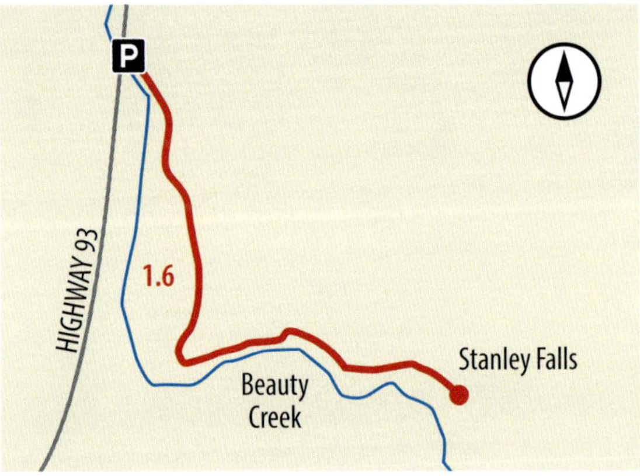

DISTANCE

3.2 km return

ELEVATION GAIN

130 m

DIFFICULTY

Easy, recommended for children aged 5 and older; good trail throughout, but there are no guard rails. Keep the little ones close by and don't let them near the edge.

SEASON

Summer and early fall

OF SPECIAL INTEREST FOR CHILDREN

The kids will love the small waterfalls and cascades as well as the bigger Stanley Falls at the end.

1. Hike the trail across Beauty Flats and turn right, onto an old road.

ABOVE, FROM LEFT One of the cascades; good parenting: Jennifer Benbow makes sure James doesn't get too close to the edge. **BELOW** Another of the waterfalls. (All three photos: Shawn Benbow.)

2. In 450 m turn left as the trail starts following Beauty Creek on its left bank. From here to the end there will be several small waterfalls and cascades to see. Watch the children carefully and hold their hands where necessary.

3. The trail goes to Stanley Falls, where the best view is just past the Stanley Falls sign. Enjoy and then return the same way you came in.

42. SUNWAPTA FALLS

A great little stop to stretch the legs and see several waterfalls.

LOCATION

Drive west on Highway 1, past Lake Louise, and take the Highway 93 turnoff (Exit 7) towards Jasper. Drive about 175 km and turn left into the Sunwapta Falls parking lot.

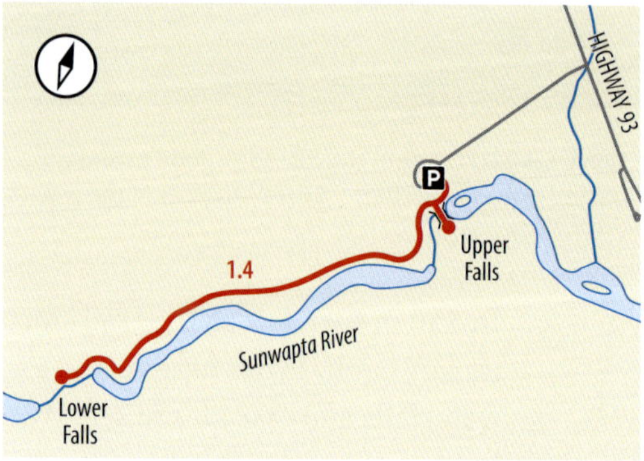

DISTANCE

2.8 km return

ELEVATION LOSS/GAIN

87 m loss/gain for the Lower Falls

DIFFICULTY

Very easy for the Upper Falls, easy for the Lower Falls, recommended for all. Good trail throughout. For safety, always stay behind the fences.

SEASON

Late spring, summer and fall.

OF SPECIAL INTEREST FOR CHILDREN

Not as spectacular as Athabasca Falls, but the hike down to the Lower Falls provides some good exercise for the young ones.

1. The Upper Falls is only minutes from the parking lot. Check it out from the bridge and both ends of the bridge, staying behind the fences.
2. The Lower Falls is easily reached via a signed trail on the north side of the Sunwapta River. Follow the descending trail as far down as the fences go and then return the same way you came in.

FOLLOWING PAGE Various views of the scenic falls (photos: Shawn Benbow).

43. ATHABASCA FALLS

A spectacular waterfall only minutes from the parking lot.

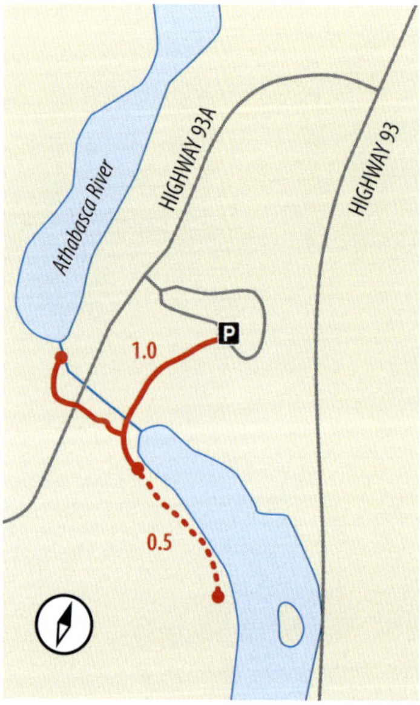

LOCATION

Drive west on Highway 1, past Lake Louise, and take the Highway 93 turnoff (Exit 7) towards Jasper. Drive about 198 km, turn left onto Highway 93A and go to the Athabasca Falls parking lot.

DISTANCE

1 km return

ELEVATION GAIN

Minimal

DIFFICULTY

Very easy, recommended for all. Excellent paved trail and some easy steps.

SEASON

Late spring, summer and fall.

OF SPECIAL INTEREST FOR CHILDREN

The kids will probably like the side trip down to the river below the falls.

1. Follow the well-marked trail to all of the viewpoints of the magnificent falls. Obviously you'll want to keep an eye on the small ones here.

2. Be sure to visit the signed "Canyon," "River" and "Pothole" for additional views.

3. Optional: To extend the trip a little, and perhaps escape the crowds, hike the trail on the other side of the river that goes upstream. Eventually the trail narrows and starts going up the embankment. This is a good place to stop, take a break and then return the same way you came in.

FROM TOP Athabasca Falls, beautifully backdropped by picturesque Mount Kerkeslin; James and Jennifer Benbow descend into the canyon; another good place for kids to observe the spectacle, which clearly impresses Walter Benbow. (All three photos: Shawn Benbow.)

Jasper

JASPER

The quaint town of Jasper is surrounded by spectacular mountain scenery and therefore a variety of wonderful hikes, many of which are appropriate for the whole family. Nearby Maligne Lake is a family favourite, featuring the easy but awe-inspiring Maligne Canyon hike and more advanced treks such as Opal Hills and Bald Hills. Just south of the townsite, the Valley of the Five Lakes is recommended for younger families.

Accommodations are plentiful in Jasper, though you'll want to book well in advance. For campers, the Wapiti, Whistler (family-oriented and highly recommended) and Snaring campgrounds provide a less expensive alternative.

Note that dogs are not allowed on the trails in Jasper, in order to protect the endangered caribou population.

FACING PAGE Jennifer, James and Shawn Benbow at the lower viewpoint of Cavell Meadows (photo: Shawn Benbow).

44. VALLEY OF THE FIVE LAKES

A great hike to five gorgeous lakes – a family favourite.

LOCATION

From Jasper, drive 8.8 km south on Highway 93 and turn left into the Valley of the Fives Lakes parking lot. If arriving from the south, the turnoff is about 21.6 km north of the turn-off to Athabasca Falls.

DISTANCE

4.5–6.4 km return

ELEVATION GAIN

112 m

DIFFICULTY

Moderate, recommended for children aged 5 and older. Good signed trail throughout. Note there are lots of ups and downs that may take a toll on young legs.

SEASON

Late spring, summer and fall.

OF SPECIAL INTEREST FOR CHILDREN

Terrific lake scenery and a few opportunities to dip your feet (or more!) in the crystal clear waters. Dogs are not allowed on this trail.

1. The trail is well signed and very easy to follow. Hike 1.1 km to a signed junction and follow the signs to First Lake.
2. Reaching First Lake, it's worth it to follow faint trails to the shoreline for a few minutes to get additional views of this beautiful lake.
3. Return to the main trail and hike to the remaining lakes, enjoying the stunning array of colours. Note that Second Lake

is prone to very low water levels. The land bridge between Third and Fourth lakes is a great place to take a break and then explore a little.

4. There is an unofficial trail circling Fifth Lake (1.9 km in length), but most choose to forgo this side trip and simply follow the loop, eventually arriving back at the signed junction. From there, return the same way you came in.

CLOCKWISE FROM TOP These Adirondack chairs are perfectly placed for viewing the magnificent Third Lake (photo: Ruzel Jamilon); the dock at Fifth Lake is a terrific spot for photos and relaxation (photo: Ruzel Jamilon); Hubert, Amélie with Amandine, and Olivia, from Quebec City, enjoying Fourth Lake.

45. PATH OF THE GLACIER / CAVELL MEADOWS

In one word: awesome!

LOCATION

From Jasper, drive 6.7 km south on Highway 93 and turn right onto Highway 93A (towards Mount Edith Cavell Road). Follow the narrow, winding road for about 14 km to its end. If arriving from the south, the turnoff is 2 km north of the turnoff to the Valley of the Five Lakes.

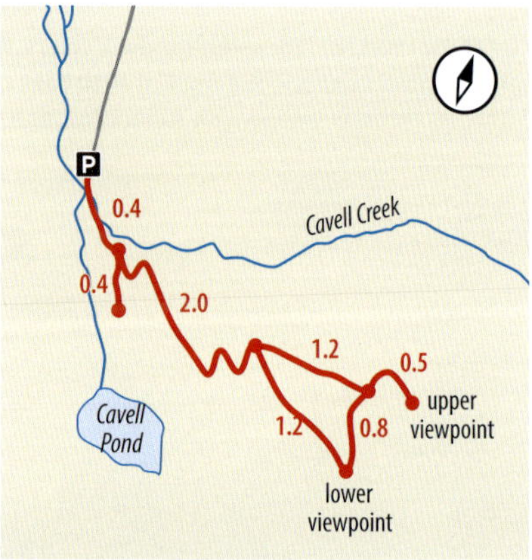

DISTANCE

8.3 km for all trails

ELEVATION GAIN

377 m; high point: 2288 m

DIFFICULTY

Strenuous, recommended for children aged 7 and older (younger children could complete the Path of the Glacier and the lower viewpoint). Good trail throughout, with several steep sections of rocky terrain.

SEASON

Summer and early fall.

OF SPECIAL INTEREST FOR CHILDREN

Close-up view of a hanging glacier and the colourful pond its meltwater creates. Dogs are not allowed on this trail.

1. Due to the excellent signage throughout, a specific route description is unnecessary. Instead, a few helpful hints are offered:
   - Complete the Path of the Glacier trail first, to a great view of Cavell Pond and Angel Glacier. Do *not* ignore the warnings about going past the barrier to get to the pond. In 2012 a huge chunk of the adjacent glacier (Ghost Glacier) calved off into the pond, and the resulting wave

CLOCKWISE FROM TOP LEFT James and Jennifer Benbow enjoy the paved trail at the beginning, with Mount Edith Cavell dominating the background; someone is up to no good; the Benbows at one of the scenic highlights of the trip. (All three photos: Shawn Benbow.)

of water decimated everything in its path, including a portion of the parking lot (which has now been relocated at a safer distance).

- For Cavell Meadows, the lower viewpoint (2118 m) offers the best view of Cavell Pond and Mount Sorrow above it (simply an outlier of Mount Edith Cavell).
- The higher viewpoint (2288 m) offers the best view of Mount Edith Cavell. This route is quite steep and a little loose in places.

46. OLD FORT POINT LOOP

If you and the family are looking for a great view of the Jasper area (with minimal effort) this route will do the trick.

LOCATION

From downtown Jasper, follow Highway 93A (Hazel Avenue) for 1 km southeast, and turn left onto Old Fort Point/Lac Beauvert Road. Follow this road for 1 km, over the Athabasca River, and turn right, into the Old Fort Point parking lot.

DISTANCE

3.7–4.2-km loop

ELEVATION GAIN

130 m; high point: 1170 m

DIFFICULTY

Moderate, recommended for children aged 5 and older. Good trail throughout, with some steep sections on descent.

SEASON

Spring, summer and fall.

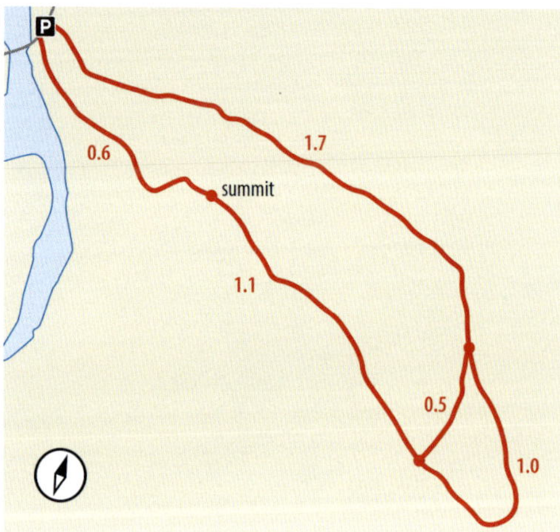

OF SPECIAL INTEREST FOR CHILDREN

The kids will love the rocky summit and the view. Do the loop in a clockwise direction so everyone gets their exercise before the pleasant summit surprise. If time and energy are limited, go counter-clockwise to the summit, then return the same way you came in. Dogs are not allowed on this trail.

1. Note the wooden staircase to the left of the trailhead kiosk – that is where you will be returning from. From the kiosk, follow the number 1 route all the way.

2. At the 1.5-km mark the trail forks. Both forks work and end up at the same place. The right fork is 0.5 km, while the left is 1.0 km and less steep. Take your pick.
3. When the trails join together, continue following the number 1 route, now heading back in the general direction of the parking lot. A couple of red Adirondack chairs provide a quick and scenic diversion along the way. The summit is an interesting rocky plateau, with open views in every direction. Spend some time here letting the kids explore, and then continue following the trail down the other side. This section is steep and extra care is warranted. Finish the trip with great views of the Athabasca River and a staircase descent.

CLOCKWISE FROM LEFT The red chairs furnish a great view of Mount Edith Cavell (photo: Brigid Meegan Scott); the Benbow boys ascend the carved-out rock steps; Walter Benbow finds a great little rest stop. (Latter two photos: Shawn Benbow.)

47. LAKE ANNETTE

Easy, scenic and ideal for families.

LOCATION

From downtown Jasper, drive north and turn onto Highway 16. Follow the signs to Maligne Lake. Once on the other side of the Athabasca River, turn right, following the signs to Lake Annette. There are many places to park that give easy access to the lake.

DISTANCE

2.4-km loop

ELEVATION GAIN

Minimal

DIFFICULTY

Very easy, recommended for all. Excellent paved and wheelchair-accessible trail around the lake.

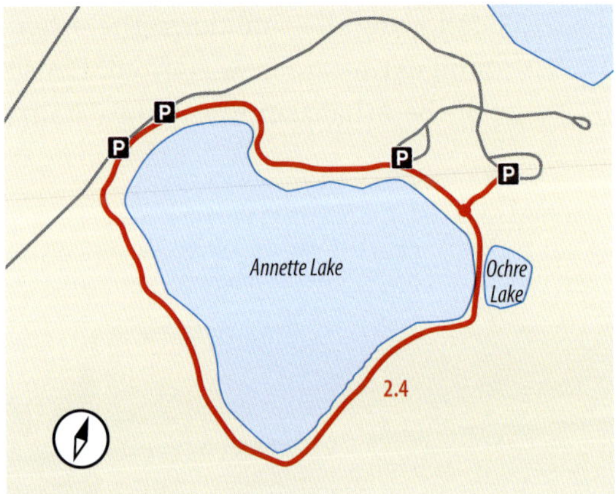

SEASON

Spring, summer and fall.

OF SPECIAL INTEREST FOR CHILDREN

Go for a swim, boat on the lake, play in the playground, but don't forget to hike around the lake! The trail is stroller-friendly. Dogs are not allowed.

1. From any of the several parking areas, find the paved trail and hike around the lake in either direction. The east side is peaceful and serene, while the north and west sides usually have more activity. There is a small beach for swimming, a dock for boat activities and a playground.

FACING PAGE FROM TOP James, Shawn, Walter and Jennifer Benbow get ready for the hike; looking across Lake Annette from the southeast shore; James Benbow has discovered something of interest on the paved trail. (All three photos: Shawn Benbow.)

48. MALIGNE CANYON

One of the premier canyons in the Canadian Rockies. Not to be missed if you are in the area.

LOCATION

From downtown Jasper, drive north and turn onto Highway 16 and follow the signs to Maligne Lake. Once on the other side of the Athabasca River, turn left, drive 6 km and turn left again into the Maligne Canyon parking lot.

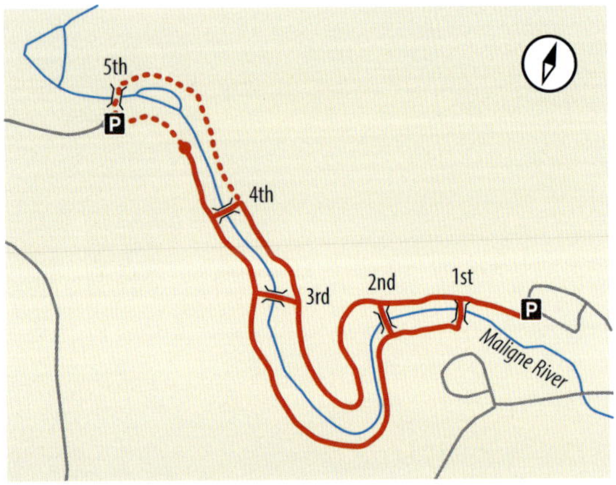

DISTANCE

1–4.4 km

ELEVATION LOSS/GAIN

50–100 m

DIFFICULTY

Easy to moderate (depending how far down you go), recommended for children aged 4 and older. Excellent trail throughout.

SEASON

Late spring, summer and early fall.

OF SPECIAL INTEREST FOR CHILDREN

Observe the power of water in the form of this stunning canyon. Dogs are not allowed on this trail.

1. No description is necessary, as the trails are well signed and easy to follow. The recommendation for families is to descend a little ways past Fourth Bridge, and then return the same way but on the opposite side of the canyon for a little variety. Fences protect very well from a fall into the canyon, but obviously you'll still want to keep an eye on the little ones. If you have two vehicles available, leave one in the Fifth Bridge parking lot and hike down to it.

FROM TOP A good opportunity to talk to the kids about the power of water erosion; the bridges offer awesome views down the canyon; the picturesque Fifth Bridge. (Middle inset and bottom photos: Shawn Benbow.)

49. OPAL HILLS

A steep forest hike to a wonderful valley and viewpoint high above Maligne Lake.

LOCATION

From downtown Jasper, drive north and turn onto Highway 16 and follow the signs to Maligne Lake. Once on the other side of the Athabasca River, turn left and drive 50 km to the lake. Upon reaching the Maligne Lake area, turn left into the first parking lot, then left again and uphill to reach the farthest of the three lots. The trail begins at the northeast corner.

DISTANCE

8.2-km loop

ELEVATION GAIN

500 m; high point: 2250 m

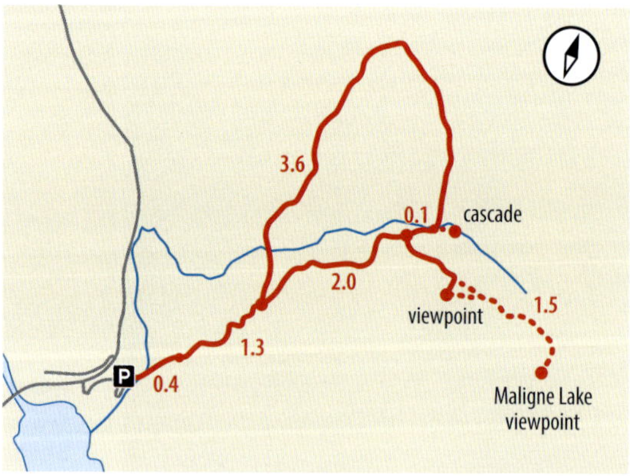

DIFFICULTY

Very strenuous, recommended for children aged 10 and older. Good but steep trail for much of the ascent.

SEASON

Summer and early fall.

OF SPECIAL INTEREST FOR CHILDREN

A quieter alternative to Bald Hills but equally strenuous. Older kids will appreciate this one. Dogs are not allowed on this trail.

1. You will be following the number 22 trail all the way. From the trailhead, hike a few hundred metres to a signed junction and take the left fork.

2. About 1.3 km of initially easy, but then relentlessly steep, hiking takes you to the next junction.

3. Take the left fork. It is longer but less steep and far more scenic. Save the other route for descent. Follow the left fork up into the valley. The trail then wraps around two hills. The big peak above you to the east is Opal Peak (a good scramble for when the kids are no longer kids). This section of the trail is 3.6 km long and eventually crosses a stream.

4. After crossing the stream you will arrive at a T-junction. Going left here takes you to a small cascade in a few hundred metres. Return to the junction if you choose this minor diversion. Going right is the continuation of trail 22.

5. Quickly you will arrive at a four-way junction. Going right here is the continuation of 22 and this is the route you will descend. However, going left and up is almost mandatory

CLOCKWISE FROM TOP LEFT James Benbow leads the hike through the scenic upper valley; the Benbows high above Maligne Lake (both upper photos: Shawn Benbow); happy hikers celebrate their achievement (photo: Explorejasper.com).

FROM TOP The vista from the Maligne viewpoint is not bad even in miserable weather; looking back at the verdant valley (photo: Shawn Benbow); snow patches can make for an exhilarating descent (photo: Explorejasper.com).

at this point. Even if you don't complete the **Going Farther** extension, it's only a short, steep hike to a wonderful view of Maligne Lake. Hike up the trail until it forks. Take the right branch and within 20 seconds you will be rewarded with that view.

6. Return to the four-way junction and hike down 22, eventually reaching the junction mentioned in step 3 above. From there, return the same way you came in.

Going Farther: Maligne Lake Viewpoint

Stunning views of the lake and surrounding mountains.

Distance

Add 3 km return

Elevation Gain

Add 280 m; high point: 2430 m

Difficulty

Very strenuous, recommended for children aged 12 and older. Good trail to start with and then faint to no trails to the summit.

1. From the four-way junction, follow the steep trail up, going east. Take either fork higher up and continue up the wide ridge.
2. The trail soon fades away. Continue going up the stable scree but trend more to the right.
3. Eventually you will see Maligne Lake Viewpoint. It is not the highest point of the ridge but an obvious grassy knoll. Make your way over there and take in the wonderful view. Return the same way you came in.

50. BALD HILLS

Little legs will get a great workout to perhaps the best view of Maligne Lake in the area.

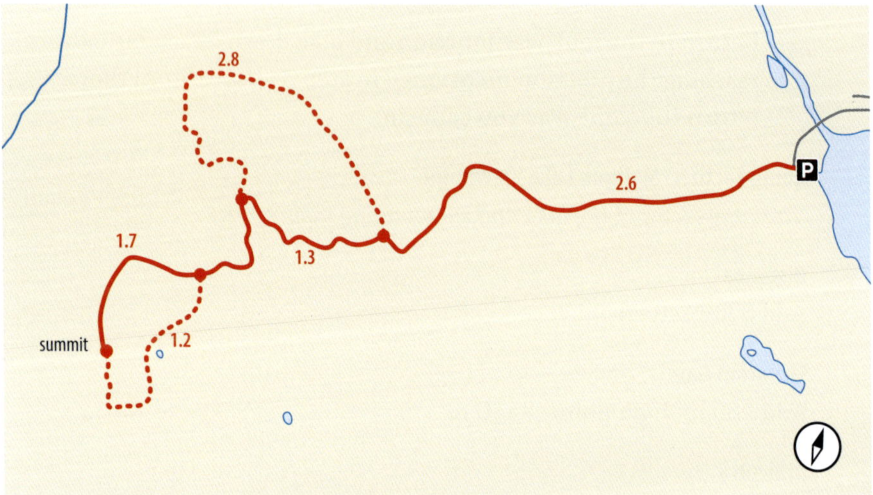

LOCATION

From downtown Jasper, drive north and turn onto Highway 16 and follow the signs to Maligne Lake. Once on the other side of the Athabasca River, turn left and drive 50 km to the lake. Upon reaching the Maligne Lake area, drive past the lake outlet and follow the signs to the Bald Hills/Skyline parking lot.

DISTANCE

13.2 km return

ELEVATION GAIN

567 m; high point: 2320 m

DIFFICULTY

Very strenuous, recommended for children aged 12 and older. Easy fire road, followed by a steep grind up a trail with lots of tree roots, then a good trail to the summit.

From near the site of the old lookout, the false summit of the objective can be seen. Note the barely visible trail going up the left side – aim for that (photo: Shawn Benbow).

SEASON

Summer and early fall.

OF SPECIAL INTEREST FOR CHILDREN

Pick a clear day so that an amazing summit view will be the reward for the kids' aching legs. Dogs are not allowed on this trail.

1. From the parking lot, cross the road and find the trailhead kiosk. Hike up the fire road for about 2.6 km.
2. At the 2.6-km mark, look for a trail on the left side of the fire road. Turn left onto that trail and follow it steeply upward for 1.3 km. (Note: You can also stay on the fire road, but this adds 1.5 km one-way to the trip).
3. At the T-junction at the top of the steep trail, turn left. The right fork goes to an open area where an old fire lookout used to be – a good place for a quick rest if the kids (or adults) need one.
4. Hike this trail for a few hundred metres, arriving at another junction. Both routes go to the summit. The left fork goes there more directly and is the one described here.

Walter and James Benbow lead the way to the summit (photo: Shawn Benbow).

5. Hike this new trail and watch for a steep, rocky path that branches off to the right and winds its way up to the top. Take this branch.
6. At the top, continue on the obvious trail to the interesting summit of Bald Hills. On a clear day the view will amaze you.
7. For the super-adventurous family, there are options to continue exploring the area to the south. Most people will choose to return the same way they came in. For some added variety on the initial part of the return trip, you can descend the south ridge until a minor trail on your left takes you back to a main trail. The return route is obvious after that.

FACING PAGE, CLOCKWISE FROM TOP The premier view of the day: a close-up of Samson Peak and Maligne Lake (photo: Shawn Benbow); hikers returning from some exploration of the high points to the south along one of the well-trodden trails (photo: Brigid Meegan Scott); the more comprehensive panorama from the top (photo: Shawn Benbow); the Benbows enjoying one of the best summits in the area (photo: Shawn Benbow).

IMPORTANT CONTACTS

Kananaskis Country Trail Reports
1.877.537.2757
albertaparks.ca/parks/kananaskis/kananaskis-country/advisories-public-safety/trail-reports/

Barrier Lake Information Centre
7 km south of Highway 1 on Highway 40
403.678.0760
albertaparks.ca/parks/kananaskis/bow-valley-pp/information-facilities/kananaskis-contacts/barrier-lake-visitor-information-centre/

Peter Lougheed Park Discovery & Information Centre
Kananaskis Trail
403.678.0760
albertaparks.ca/parks/kananaskis/peter-lougheed-pp/information-facilities/kananaskis-contacts/peter-lougheed-park-discovery-information-centre/

Banff National Park Information Centre
224 Banff Avenue, Banff
403.762.1550
pc.gc.ca/en/pn-np/ab/banff/visit

Lake Louise Visitor Centre
201 Village Rd., next to Samson Mall, Lake Louise
403.522.3833
pc.gc.ca/en/pn-np/ab/banff/visit

Yoho Visitor Centre
Field, BC
250.343.6783
pc.gc.ca/en/pn-np/bc/yoho

Family fun at Parker Ridge (photo: Shawn Benbow).

Jasper Visitor Centre

500 Connaught Drive, Jasper
780.852.6176
Backcountry trail office: 780-852-6177
pc.gc.ca/en/pn-np/ab/jasper/visit/heures-hours

Emergency

Dial 911

Moraine Lake: world renowned and deservedly so.

ACKNOWLEDGEMENTS

Once again a huge thank you to Tanya Koob, for photos, invaluable information and inspiration. Thank you to Gillean and Tony Daffern for paving the way for so many of us in the Canadian Rockies. Also to Lynda Pianosi and Brenda Kurtz Lenko for authoring their family hiking guidebooks. And thank you to the following individuals for their photo contributions: Jennifer Benbow, Shawn Benbow, Connie Biggart, Par Boora, Matthew Clay, Chris Doering, Mark Fioretti, Gordon Hobbs, Matthew Hobbs, Greg Jones, Stacey Jones, Melissa Kindt, Denise Kitagawa and family, Mark Koob, Nicole Lisafeld, Leigh McAdam, Mark Nugara, Brigid Meegan Scott, Christian Skogen, Amélie Stavric, Marko Stavric, Karen Ung, Kheang Ung, Amy Wong and Eddie Wong.

Special thanks to Shawn Benbow for his photo-editing expertise.

DISCLAIMER

There are inherent risks in hiking mountain areas that require hikers to constantly use their own judgment. Anyone using this book does so at their own risk, and both the author and the publisher disclaim any liability for any injuries or other damage that may be sustained by anyone hiking any of the trails described in this book.

Be aware that bear sightings and fire hazard can close trails at a moment's notice. Flash floods can wash out bridges. Fallen trees resulting from strong winds can block trails and make the going difficult.

In this book there are no dos and don'ts. It is assumed that users are caring, intelligent people who will respect the country they are travelling through and its wildlife.

ABOVE Noah Koob hikes through a patch of wildflowers at Sunshine Meadows (photo: Tanya Koob). **FOLLOWING SPREAD** Emerald Lake is popular for good reason.

19
8

Eiffel Lake, with the world-famous Valley of the Ten Peaks as a stunning background.